CAMPAIGN 315

THE HINDENBURG LINE 1918

Haig's forgotten triumph

ALISTAIR MCCLUSKEY

ILLUSTRATED BY PETER DENNIS

Series editor Marcus Cowper

Osprey Publishing
c/o Bloomsbury Publishing Plc
PO Box 883, Oxford, OX1 9PL, UK
Or
c/o Bloomsbury Publishing Inc.
1385 Broadway, 5th Floor, New York, NY 10018, USA
E-mail: info@ospreypublishing.com

www.ospreypublishing.com

OSPREY is a trademark of Osprey Publishing Ltd, a division of Bloomsbury
Publishing Plc.

First published in Great Britain in 2017

© 2017 Osprey Publishing Ltd

A CIP catalogue record for this book is available from the British Library.

ISBN: PB: 9781472820303
            ePub: 9781472820327
            ePDF: 9781472820310
            XML: 9781472822758

17 18 19 20 21   10 9 8 7 6 5 4 3 2 1

Editorial by Ilios Publishing Ltd (http://www.iliospublishing.com)
Index by Alison Worthington
Typeset in Myriad Pro and Sabon
Maps by Bounford.com
3D BEVs by The Black Spot
Page layouts by PDQ Digital Media Solutions, Bungay, UK
Printed in China through World Print Ltd

Osprey Publishing supports the Woodland Trust, the UK's leading woodland
conservation charity. Between 2014 and 2018 our donations are being
spent on their Centenary Woods project in the UK.

To find out more about our authors and books visit **www.
ospreypublishing.com**. Here you will find extracts, author interviews,
details of forthcoming events and the option to sign up for our newsletter.

ACKNOWLEDGMENTS

This book could not have been written without the help and support of
many friends and colleagues. In particular I would like to thank, Professors
Gary Sheffield and Stephen Badsey; Drs Jonathan Boff, Stuart Mitchell,
Matthias Strohn, Stephen Walsh and Tim Gale; Mr Andrew Orgill and his
staff at the RMA Sandhurst Library and Marcus Cowper and the team at
Osprey. All listened patiently to my ideas and provided wise counsel where
necessary; all errors that may remain are my own. Thanks to Peter Dennis
and the graphics team at Bounford for bringing my text to life.
Most of all I would like to thank Sue and Ben who once again tolerated a
husband and father AWOL in the archives or drawing maps. Without your
love and support this project could never have been completed. Finally,
this book is dedicated to two of Ben's great grandfathers – Sgt. FF Ridge, RE,
HQ 18th (Eastern) Division and 2Lt. JE Hand, an original member of the
46th (North Midland) Division – together with the soldiers, sailors and
airmen of all nations who fought in this epic battle.

ARTIST'S NOTE

Readers may care to note that the original paintings from which the colour
plates in this book were prepared are available for private sale. All
reproduction copyright whatsoever is retained by the Publishers. All
enquiries should be addressed to:

Peter Dennis, Fieldhead, The Park. Mansfield, Notts, NG18 2AT, UK
Email: magie.h@ntlworld.com

The Publishers regret that they can enter into no correspondence upon
this matter.

IMPERIAL WAR MUSEUMS COLLECTIONS

Many of the photos in this book come from the huge collections of IWM
(Imperial War Museums) which cover all aspects of conflict involving Britain
and the Commonwealth since the start of the twentieth century. These
rich resources are available online to search, browse and buy at www.iwm.org.
uk/collections. In addition to Collections Online, you can visit the Visitor
Rooms where you can explore over 8 million photographs, thousands of
hours of moving images, the largest sound archive of its kind in the world,
thousands of diaries and letters written by people in wartime, and a huge
reference library. To make an appointment, call (020) 7416 5320, or e-mail
mail@iwm.org.uk
Imperial War Museums www.iwm.org.uk

Key to military symbols

Army Group	Army	Corps	Division	Brigade	Regiment	Battalion
Company/Battery	Platoon	Section	Squad	Infantry	Artillery	Cavalry
Airborne	Unit HQ	Air defense	Air Force	Air mobile	Air transportable	Amphibious
Antitank	Armor	Air aviation	Bridging	Engineer	Headquarters	Maintenance
Medical	Missile	Mountain	Navy	Nuclear, biological, chemical	Ordnance	Parachute
Reconnaissance	Signal	Supply	Transport movement	Rocket artillery	Air defense artillery	

Key to unit identification

Unit identifier | Parent unit
Commander
(+) with added elements
(-) less elements

CONTENTS

The General Offensive

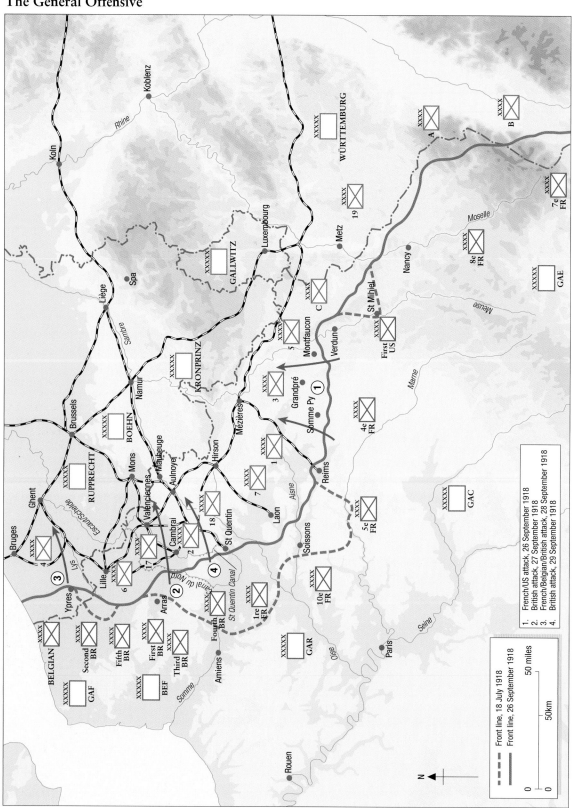

Front line, 18 July 1918
Front line, 26 September 1918

1. French/US attack, 26 September 1918
2. British attack, 27 September 1918
3. French/Belgian/British attack, 28 September 1918
4. British attack, 29 September 1918

THE STRATEGIC SITUATION

Between 26 and 29 September 1918, the Allies launched their largest combined attack on the Western Front during World War I. As part of Maréchal Foch's General Offensive, the British, French, American and Belgian armies launched four attacks in rapid succession across a 350km front between the Argonne and Flanders. At the centre of this huge assault the British Expeditionary Force's (BEF) First, Third and Fourth Armies, supported by the French 1re Armée, breached the formidable Hindenburg Line defences between Cambrai and St Quentin. In stark contrast to the bloody stalemates of 1916–17, this success drove the German Army from its last fully prepared defensive position west of the Rhine, shattering the authority of the German Imperial and military establishment. However, while this battle demonstrated the newly found tactical and operational dominance of the Allies, it also exposed the latent strategic tensions between them as they sought the most advantageous positions for the post-war settlement. These factors converged to ensure that, as a result, the Armistice with Germany was imposed in 1918 and on stringent Allied terms. From 1918 onwards, however, the battle of the Hindenburg Line struggled to receive the public recognition it deserved and, unlike the Somme and Passchendaele, soon slipped from the cultural memory of the war. It became Haig's forgotten triumph.

The German Army constructed the Hindenburg Line in response to the unsustainable casualty rates it suffered in 1916 at Verdun and on the Somme. When Hindenburg and Ludendorff replaced Falkenhayn as leaders of the German Supreme Command – Oberste Heeresleitung (OHL) – in early September, they immediately reviewed the Central Powers' strategy. As a result, the German Army assumed a defensive posture in France and Flanders and the main strategic offensive in the West transferred to the German Navy, which prepared to launch a submarine campaign against Allied shipping in 1917. This strategy required the construction of a state-of-the-art defensive position between Arras and Laon, which shortened the front line by approximately 45km, releasing units to reconstitute the German reserve, and also implemented all the lessons learnt during 1915–16 in how to fight effective defensive battles. The new position provided deep

German dead outside a dugout on the Somme in 1916. The German Army suffered around 700,000 casualties here and at Verdun under the crushing weight of Allied artillery fire. This experience was a major factor in the decision to build a defence line that was both difficult for the British and French guns to hit and protected the garrison from blast and shrapnel when in their fighting positions. (IWM, Q4256)

The Hindenburg Line at Inchy-en-Artois. The belts of barbed wire and the parallel trench lines running across the centre of photograph were a signature feature of the German defensive systems of 1917–18. (IWM, Q58649)

shelters and trenches to protect the front-line troops, who in turn used thick obstacle belts integrated with fire-swept zones to block Allied thrusts. The Germans named the new line the Siegfried Stellung after the mythological hero, but it was quickly christened 'The Hindenburg Line' by the Allies after its presumed creator. A workforce of 65,000 men began construction in late September 1916 and by March 1917 it was complete. Three further defence lines were developed from it in quick succession. The Wotan Stellung ran north from Arras to Lille. Meanwhile, the Hunding-Brunhild-Kriemhild Stellung ran south-east from Laon to Verdun, while the Michael Stellung ran across the base of the St Mihiel salient. Together they formed a shield from the North Sea, via Arras, Soissons and Verdun, to Metz.

The Siegfried Stellung eventually consisted of up to four defence lines arranged in a zone 4 miles deep. These became known to the Allies as the 'Advanced Hindenburg Line', the 'Main Hindenburg Line', the 'Hindenburg Support Line' and the 'Hindenburg Reserve Line'. In the sector between Cambrai and St Quentin, each ran broadly north to south with approximately 2,500m separation between them. Where specific areas of threat were identified, additional trenches were added, such as the 'Marcoing Line' and 'Cantaing Line' near Cambrai. Separately from the nomenclature outlined above, sections of each line could be named after localities at either end of them, such as the 'Masnieres–Beaurevoir–Fonsommes Line' also being used for the 'Hindenburg Reserve Line' between these villages. Between Cambrai and St Quentin, these lines exploited the Canal du Nord and the St Quentin Canal to provide additional obstacles. The former was under construction at the outbreak of the war and was mostly dry. The latter was built by Napoleon's engineers and included the 6km-long Bellicourt Tunnel, passing under the watershed between the river Schelde and the river Somme. The forward trenches of the Main Hindenburg Line generally ran along the eastern bank of both canals where their paths converged, and ran north-west to south-east between Havrincourt and Bantouzelle to pass from one canal to the other. At the Bellicourt Tunnel, the Main Hindenburg Line defences swept to the west of the canal line to protect the de facto 'bridge' it provided, while barges in the tunnel itself also acted as shell-proof underground accommodation for the garrison. Each canal was faced with brick walls up to 3m high, and while the older St Quentin Canal (known as the Schelde Canal by the BEF north of the Bellicourt Tunnel in 1918) was around 11m wide, the more modern Canal du Nord was excavated to a width of up to 40m. Concrete dams had been constructed by the Germans to retain water in certain sectors while elsewhere deep mud prevailed. Wire entanglements were inserted into both. Where the canals crossed the rolling chalk downs between Cambrai and St Quentin, cuttings 15–25m deep existed to enhance their value as military obstacles. Two further tunnel systems existed in addition to that at Bellicourt. At Bellenglise a tunnel had been mined into the hillside behind the Hindenburg Main position to shelter approximately 3,000 men, while further south, the Le Tronquoy Tunnel carried the canal under the high ground 5km north of St Quentin. South of St Quentin the line ran along the eastern bank of the river Oise, exploiting the river and its wide marsh-filled valley as a major obstacle to any Allied attack.

By the end of 1917, the strategic situation had changed dramatically. The collapse of Tsarist Russia, and the advantage gained over Italy after the battle of Caporetto, enabled Germany to re-consider offensive operations on the Western Front once again. Here they now held the initiative over the French and British, whose armies were recuperating following the punishing Nivelle Offensive and the Third Ypres campaigns. This strategic opportunity was counterbalanced by the growing threat from the United States, which had entered the war in April 1917 as an Associated Power to the Entente, in response to Germany's unrestricted submarine warfare. Although somewhat raw in skill and dependent on British and French industry for the majority of their equipment, the increasing strength of the American Expeditionary Force (AEF) only promised to shift the initiative back towards the Allies from the middle of 1918 onwards. Consequently, sensing a six-month window of opportunity, on 21 January OHL ordered the launching of a series of massive assaults designed to defeat Britain and France before American strength could be brought to bear.

A reinforced concrete dugout entrance in the Hindenburg Line. These shelters were essential to protect the German front-line troops from the weight of Allied artillery. (IWM, E(AUS) 3581)

In March 1918, the first of these blows saw the Hindenburg Line between Arras and St Quentin act as the springboard for the German attempt to destroy the BEF. Operation *Michael* saw the 17., 2. and 18. Armeen drive back the British Third and Fifth Armies an unprecedented 40 miles in 15 days of bitter fighting. Further assaults were launched in Flanders in April, on the Aisne in May, on the Matz in June and on the Marne in July, all of which also captured much ground and imposed heavy casualties on the Allies. However, although severely stretched, the Allied line held, and in the process exacted a huge toll from the Germans. Although the British and French suffered 288,000 and 225,000 casualties between March and the end of June, the German Army lost a staggering 688,000 men during the same period.

American infantry marching to the docks at Southampton for embarkation. Although Russia had been knocked out of the war, the prospect of American forces flooding into France during 1918 was a key factor in the German decision to launch a pre-emptive attempt to secure victory through the Spring Offensives. (IWM, Q70817)

These casualty rates fundamentally shaped the political context, where much trepidation remained in the Allied governments over the critical manpower shortages for the coming battles. The crippling human cost since 1914 resulted in both the British and French politicians developing plans for the war's culminating campaigns to be fought in 1919 on the back of American troops now flooding into France. In Britain, the War Cabinet deliberated the future British strategy together with the Dominion governments. The Prime Minister, Lloyd George, wanted a return to an 'eastern' strategy to maximize Britain's post-

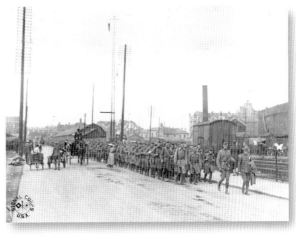

war Imperial benefits. He argued for manpower to be prioritized into the Royal Navy and industry, particularly shipbuilding, at the expense of the BEF which was to be reduced in size. He was supported to some extent by the General Staff at the War Office, but even General Henry Wilson, the Chief of the Imperial General Staff (CIGS) and Billy Hughes, the Australian Prime Minister, pointed out that the war would only be won by defeating the German Army and that this would have to be done in France. On 16 August, the Cabinet agreed the compromise strategy to prepare the BEF to fight alongside the French and Americans on the Western Front in 1919 but with an army lavishly supplied with guns and tanks to offset the diminishing manpower base. Although these debates took place as the Allied fortunes improved following the battles on the Marne and at Amiens, the Cabinet's fear of repeating the heavy casualties of the 1916–17 campaigns was deeply rooted. Consequently, on 31 August General Wilson sent Haig a telegram highlighting the risks that would be associated with a costly but unsuccessful attack on the Hindenburg Line. Unsurprisingly, Haig was furious at the lack of support he now felt he was receiving from London, describing the Cabinet as a 'wretched lot' in his reply to Wilson. Nevertheless, he travelled to London to reassure Milner, the Secretary of State for War, and to plead for more manpower to sustain the BEF. However, although Haig believed he had been well received, in private both Milner and Wilson feared 'another Passchendaele', with Milner stating that if Haig 'broke' the current BEF, there would be no other to replace it.

Although the tensions between the French military and politicians were not as great as those the British faced, the French Army's offensive capabilities were still fragile after three years of heavy losses despite its rehabilitation under Pétain, the French Chief of the General Staff. Notwithstanding the significant French-led victory on the Marne, on 31 July he warned Foch, the Allied Supreme Military Commander, that the French Army was now at the 'limit of effort', being over 100,000 men under establishment. As a result, Foch requested that the men due for conscription in 1920 be called up two years early, in 1918. The French Government agreed but with Prime Minister Clemenceau's caveat that French blood was now the 'most precious material' and was to be conserved where possible.

British and French infantry fighting in the Bois de Reims, 23 July 1918, during the second battle of the Marne. The appointment of Foch as Supreme Military Commander at Doullens on 26 March 1918 greatly improved the cooperation and coordination between the Allied armies. Most of the major engagements saw one country's reserves supporting forces from another when required. This was an essential improvement in the Allied effort to defeat the German Army on the Western Front. (IWM, Q11110)

The German Army was also suffering a manpower crisis. In April 1918 it had 4,000,000 men on the Western Front and 1,000,000 on the Eastern Front. Casualty replacements for the West were provided in part by sick and wounded returning to duty, combing out rear area units and further redeployment of men from Russia. However, by July the army in the West had been reduced in strength to 3,580,000 and in the East down to 580,000. In response, Germany also called up their 1920 recruit class, which was expected to provide around 300,000 troops, but these would not be ready for deployment until the autumn on completion of their training. However, the scale of the casualties was too great for even these measures. Consequently, the combat strength of front-line battalions could only be sustained by disbanding 22 infantry divisions and redistributing their manpower.

Notwithstanding its manpower difficulties, Germany was also beginning to polarize politically. In response to the failure of the unrestricted submarine campaign, the centre and left-wing parties in the Reichstag formed a majority coalition on a 'peace without annexations' mandate. This majority was held in check for the time being by the right-wing minority, the Kaiser and OHL, who remained empowered following the victory over Tsarist Russia and the advances in the West. The situation was exacerbated by the tightening grip of the Allied naval blockade, which saw Germany's civilian population slide towards starvation. Any potential source of relief from the East had proved too small in scale, as Germany was forced to balance the conflicting interests of the Bolshevik and Ukrainian regimes that blocked efficient access to the harvest. OHL desperately needed time to replenish the western armies and develop a stable and economically productive situation in Eastern Europe to support the German Empire.

From the middle of July, as the Allies regained the initiative, the Hindenburg Line reassumed its pivotal role in both the Allied and German plans. On 24 July, Foch issued a strategic directive to drive the German forces from France and Belgium in three phases. First, the main railways in Allied possession were to be secured from German threat and the Germans pushed back to the defensive positions they held at the turn of the year. Second, a combined offensive was to break through these positions. Third, the Germans were to be cleared from France and Belgium. In response, Ludendorff planned to exhaust the Allies, successfully arguing against the Foreign Minister, Admiral von Hintze, at an Imperial Council at Spa on 14 August, that repeating the successful defensive battles of 1917 together with some limited offensives could deliver a negotiated settlement. But rather than withdrawing to the Hindenburg Line immediately, as argued by some senior members of the General Staff, Ludendorff could not bring himself to voluntarily surrender the ground bought with so much blood, consequently ordering the occupation of an extemporized 'Winter Line' running north–south from Noyon to Queant and anchored on the River Somme. However, events on the battlefield were now gathering their own momentum. Spearheaded by the Fourth Army, the BEF's rapid successes during August pushed the Germans back across the old Somme battlefield, and on 31 August, the Australian Corps ruptured the German 'Winter Line' with a dramatic *coup de main* at Mont St Quentin north of Péronne. Faced with simultaneous pressure from the British First Army beginning to push south-eastwards from Arras, Ludendorff had little alternative than to order the further withdrawal back to the Hindenburg Line itself setting the scene for the climactic engagement.

An Australian soldier in the street fighting in Péronne, 3 September 1918. Although the Western Front is forever associated with trench combat, during the General Offensive much of the BEF's fighting took place in villages as they fought the Germans for control of key transport routes or tactically dominating ground. (IWM, Q11271)

CHRONOLOGY

21 March	Operation *Michael* commences. Germans advance west from the Hindenburg Line.
5 April	Operation *Michael* finishes with front line east of Amiens.
8 August	Battles of Amiens (British Fourth Army) and Montdidier begin.
11 August	Battle of Amiens ends.
15 August	Battle of Montdidier ends.
21 August	Battle of Albert 1918 (British Third Army) begins.
22 August	Battle of the Scarpe 1918 (British First Army) begins.
27 August	Haig's letter to Foch recommending the shift of American effort from Metz to Meziérès to complement British thrust on Cambrai–St Quentin.
29 August	Battle of Albert 1918 ends.
30 August	Battle of the Scarpe 1918 ends. Second battle of Bapaume (British Third Army) begins.
1 September	Mont St Quentin and Péronne captured (British Fourth Army).
2 September	Battle of the Drocourt-Quéant Line (British First Army). German withdrawal to the Hindenburg Line begins.
3 September	Second battle of Bapaume ends. Foch issues Operational Directive to breach the Hindenburg Line.
4 September	Pursuit to the Hindenburg Line begins.
6 September	OHL Conference at Avesnes decides to fight on the Hindenburg Line.
8 September	Haig requests opinions of Horne, Byng and Rawlinson over the Hindenburg Line assault.
9 September	Foch adds Flanders attack to his Operational Directive.
12 September	Battle of Havrincourt (British Third Army) (First Battle of the Hindenburg Line). Battle of St Mihiel (American First Army).
15 September	Horne and Byng commence planning for assault on the Main Hindenburg Line.
18 September	Battle of Épehy (British Fourth Army). Rawlinson commences planning for assault on the Main Hindenburg Line.

23 September	Foch issues final dates for synchronized assaults starting on 26 September.
26 September	Franco-American Argonne Offensive begins.
27 September	Battle of the Canal du Nord begins.
28 September	Battle of Ypres 1918 begins.
29 September	Battle of St Quentin begins.
1 October	Battle of the Canal du Nord ends.
2 October	Battles of St Quentin Canal and Ypres 1918 end.
3 October	Battle of the Beaurevoir Line begins.
5 October	Battle of the Beaurevoir Line ends.
8 October	Battle of Cambrai 1918 begins.
9 October	Battle of Cambrai 1918 ends (Final Battle of the Hindenburg Line).
17 October	Battle of the Selle begins (British First, Third and Fourth Armies).
25 October	Battle of the Selle ends.
1 November	Battle of Valenciennes (British First and Third Armies).
4 November	Battle of the Sambre (British Fourth Army).
6 November	Sedan liberated.
8 November	Mauberge liberated.
11 November	Mons liberated and Armistice.

OPPOSING COMMANDERS

ALLIED COMMANDERS

Maréchal Ferdinand Foch was an artilleryman who had spent the vast majority of his pre-war career in staff appointments, culminating in 1908 as Commandant of the École Supérieure de Guerre. He led XX Corps through the frontier battles of 1914 before promotion to command 9e Armée on the Marne, and subsequently the Groupe d'Armées du Nord (GAN) through the Artois battles of 1915. His star waned somewhat following the Somme campaign in 1916 before he re-emerged as Chief of the General Staff of the Army in May 1917. By 1918 he had shown himself to be an effective manager of civil–military relations when he was summoned on 26 March to take over the role as Generalissimo of the Allied Forces in the face of the German onslaught. Throughout the war he demonstrated an energetic determination to drive his subordinates to better efforts on the front line. This was increasingly tempered with a reflective ability that underpinned his adept handling of political and military leaders in meeting the challenges posed by the German Army.

Haig and his army commanders. Plumer is front left with Rawlinson front right. In the second row, Byng is on the left, Munro is in the centre and Birdwood is on the right. (IWM, Q9689)

Field Marshal Sir Douglas Haig commanded the BEF. A career cavalryman, he began the war in command of I Corps in 1914, before moving to First Army in 1915. Following the disaster at Loos in October he succeeded Sir John French as CinC of the BEF. He led the Army through the trials of the Somme, Arras and Third Ypres and oversaw its transition to a citizen conscript force from its Regular and Reservist foundations. Although he had a reputation for being a poor verbal communicator, British politicians were more suspicious of what they viewed as over optimism and questionable military judgement. However, having almost lost his post during the German Offensives in 1918, his support of Foch's appointment as Generalissimo and his subsequent performance managing both him and his subordinate army commanders suggest an individual who was becoming increasingly effective as a strategic and operational level leader.

First Army was commanded by **General Sir Henry Horne**. He led the artillery of I Corps through 1914 before taking over command of 2nd Division in early 1915. In November he accompanied Kitchener to the Dardanelles and by early 1916 had been appointed to command XV Corps in Egypt. In April he was recalled to France and reformed XV Corps as part of Rawlinson's Fourth Army on the Somme. In October he was promoted to command First Army with which he oversaw the capture of Vimy Ridge in April 1917. He held this critical position and the Arras sector through the course of the German Spring Offensives in 1918. His combat performance throughout these appointments marked Horne as a consummate tactician. He was particularly effective in using firepower and other technology to assist his men and in exploiting the terrain in manoeuvring his force to advantage.

Lieutenant-General Sir Arthur Currie, GOC Canadian Corps. (IWM, CO1970)

Horne's corps commanders in the Hindenburg Line battle were Lieutenant-Generals **Sir Alexander Godley** of XXII Corps and **Sir Arthur Currie** of the Canadian Corps. Although a British officer, Godley began the War as Commandant of the New Zealand Military Forces. He led the composite Australian-New Zealand Division and Corps at Gallipoli before arriving in France in 1916. He fought on the Somme and at Ypres before the II ANZAC Corps was re-designated XXII Corps in 1918. Currie was a member of the militia before mobilizing to command a brigade at Ypres in 1915 and a division on the Somme and Arras in 1916–17. He was promoted to command the Canadian Corps for the battle of Third Ypres. He developed the reputation for thorough and pragmatic plans that maximized the use of firepower.

Lieutenant-General Sir Charles Fergusson, GOC XVII Corps. (IWM, HU122006)

Third Army was commanded by **General Sir Julian Byng**. Byng commanded 3rd Cavalry Division at Antwerp and Ypres in 1914 and early 1915. In May he assumed command of the Cavalry Corps before moving to Gallipoli in August to take over IX Corps at Suvla. After a brief period in command of the Suez defences in January 1916, he returned to the Western Front to lead XVII Corps at Arras. In May he was appointed to command the Canadian Corps and led them through the bitter autumn fighting on the Somme and the hard-won success at Vimy in April 1917. In June he was promoted to command Third Army and planned the ground-breaking attack at Cambrai with a predicted artillery barrage and massed armoured and infantry assault. In March 1918 he held his army together in the face of the Spring Offensive before breaking the back of the critical German assault on Arras.

Byng's corps commanders were Lieutenant-Generals **Sir Charles Fergusson** of XVII Corps, **Sir Aylmer Haldane** of VI Corps, **Sir George Harper** of IV Corps, and **Sir Cameron Shute** of V Corps. Fergusson commanded 5th and then 9th Divisions in 1914, seeing combat at Le Cateau and on the Aisne. In January 1915 he took over II Corps before moving to XVII Corps in May 1916, where he remained until the end of the war. Haldane commanded 3rd Division from the outbreak of the war until 1916, when he took over VI Corps. Harper was staff officer in GHQ before assuming command of 51st Highland Division in September 1915, and leading it through the battles of the Somme, Arras, Third Ypres and Cambrai. In March 1918 he moved to IV Corps. Shute commanded 59th Brigade in 1915 before leading in turn 63rd (Royal Naval), 32nd and 19th Divisions through 1916–17. In April 1918 he assumed command of V Corps.

At the head of Fourth Army was **General Sir Henry Rawlinson**. Rawlinson was an infantry officer who briefly commanded 4th Division on the Aisne in September 1914 before leading IV Corps at Ypres, Neuve Chapelle and Loos. In January 1916 he assumed command of the newly formed Fourth Army for the Somme Offensive, but disappointing results saw him 'sidelined' during 1917 before moving to the Supreme War Council in January 1918. In March he replaced Hubert Gough in command of Fifth Army in the latter stages of Operation *Michael* and successfully defended Amiens from the final German assaults. He then oversaw the renaming of his force as Fourth Army and its rehabilitation through the summer, culminating in the successful attack at Amiens on 8 August. Rawlinson was a capable professional who repeatedly demonstrated pragmatic and practical solutions to the tasks faced by his men. By 1918, however, he had also developed the self-confidence to back his judgement against Haig's in a manner that had eluded him in 1916.

Rawlinson's corps commanders were Lieutenant-Generals **Sir Richard Butler** of III Corps, **Sir John Monash** of the Australian Corps and **Sir Walter Braithwaite** of IX Corps. Attached to Fourth Army was also **Major-General George Read** of II (US) Corps, which fought alongside Monash's Australians. Butler spent much of the war in staff appointments in I Corps, First Army and GHQ. His offhand manner towards field commanders such as Rawlinson in this period was a source of lingering irritation. His operational command was limited, having assumed command of III Corps in January 1918, and he did not hold Rawlinson's confidence. Monash was a civil engineer by profession and was a member of the militia before

Lieutenant-General Sir John Monash, GOC Australian Corps. (IWM, E(AUS)2350)

the war. He served as a brigade commander in Gallipoli and as a divisional commander on the Western Front. He took over the Australian Corps in June 1918, where he developed the reputation as cool and effective in combat. Braithwaite began the war in a staff appointment in the War Office, before deploying to Gallipoli as the Mediterranean Expeditionary Force (MEF) Chief of Staff. Loathed by the Australians in particular for his perceived arrogance, his indifferent performance saw him recalled to London. In January 1917 he was assigned to command 62nd Division, which he led at Arras and against the German Spring Offensive at Bullecourt and Cambrai. He took over IX Corps on 13 September. Read saw action in the US–Mexican border campaign in 1916 before returning to Washington as a member of the Army General Staff. In April 1918, after a brief period in command of 15th Cavalry Division, he moved to 30th Infantry Division, which he took to France. In June he assumed command of II (US) Corps in preparation for the coming offensive.

In GHQ Reserve were the Cavalry Corps commanded by Lieutenant-General **Sir Charles Kavanagh** and XIII Corps commanded by Lieutenant-General **Sir Tom Morland**. Kavanagh commanded 7th Cavalry Brigade in 1914 and, from April 1915, 2nd Cavalry Division. He moved to 5th Division in July 1915 where he remained until taking over the Cavalry Corps in 1917. Morland commanded 5th Division at Ypres in 1914 before taking over X Corps in 1915, which he led on the Somme in 1916 and Messines in 1917. He moved to XIII Corps in 1918.

Supporting the British between St Quentin and the Oise was the French 1re Armée, part of the Groupe d'Armées Réserve (GAR). GAR was commanded by **Général Émile Fayolle**. Fayolle commanded a division at the Marne in 1914 and 33e Corps in Artois in 1915, before taking over 6e Armée on the Somme in 1916. In April 1917 he was promoted to command Groupe d'Armées Centre (GAC), before taking over GAR in March 1918. **Général Eugène Debeney** commanded the French 1re Armée. Debeney began the war as the Chief of Staff of 1re Armée before being promoted to command 25e Division d'infanterie and seeing action at Verdun in early 1916. He commanded 32e Corps on the Somme in April, before a further promotion to command 7e Armée in December 1916. A year later he returned to command 1re Armée, successfully halting the German Offensive between Amiens and Montdidier in March, before taking part in the August counter-offensive in the same sector. Acutely aware of the human cost borne by the French Army since 1914, his tactical approach primarily relied on firepower to avoid overextending the endurance of his men.

Debeney's Corps Commanders were **Général de Riols de Fonclare** of 15e Corps, **Général Nollet** of 36e Corps, **Général Toulorge** of 31e Corps and **Général Hély d'Oissel** of 8e Corps, who played a peripheral role in the battle. De Fonclare commanded 1re Division d'infanterie at Verdun and on the Somme in 1916, where he was promoted to command 33e Corps. In 1917 he took over 35e Corps at Verdun until it redeployed to Picardy in summer 1918 for the counter-offensive. Nollet commanded 129e and 66e Divisions d'infanterie in Alsace, Lorraine and Champagne in 1915. He took over 12e Corps at Verdun in 1916, before moving to 36e Corps on the Channel coast in March 1917. The corps fought on the Avre and in Flanders during the German Spring Offensive in March 1918 and moved back to Picardy in September. Toulorge commanded 27e and 130e Divisions d'infanterie between January 1916 and February 1918, seeing heavy fighting at Verdun. He moved to 31e Corps in February 1918, fighting at Villers-Brettoneaux in April and at Montdidier in August.

GERMAN COMMANDERS

The de facto operational commander at OHL was **General Erich Ludendorff.** Ludendorff began the war as Deputy Chief of Staff of the Second Army and won national recognition for his role in the capture of the frontier fortresses around Liège in August 1914. He was rapidly deployed to successfully defend East Prussia as Hindenburg's Chief of Staff at 8. Armee before leading it through the Gorlice–Tarnów counter-offensive in 1915. In 1916 he followed Hindenburg to OHL, assuming the position of 'First Quartermaster General'. This shift into the grand strategic environment saw Ludendorff develop increasingly extreme nationalistic objectives. He proposed widespread annexations in the East to implement the Treaty of Brest-Litovsk, and also in the West, where even after the defeat of his Spring Offensive in the summer of 1918, he sought opportunities to retain German control of the occupied parts of France and Belgium. He retained tight operational and tactical control over the German armies, giving limited freedom of action to his army group commanders. This undermined his ability to work effectively with them.

The German forces west of Cambrai formed the left wing of Heeresgruppe Rupprecht, commanded by **Kronprinz Rupprecht of Bavaria.** Rupprecht was a professional soldier who commanded 6. Armee in Lorraine and Flanders in 1914–15. He was appointed to lead the northernmost Heeresgruppe through the defensive battles on the Somme, at Arras and at Third Ypres in 1916–17. He possessed better military insight than most of his peers and proved himself to be a shrewd and effective commander. However, his failure to secure Arras and Ypres-Hazebrouck during the 1918 Spring Offensive and his army group being surprised at Amiens in August showed he was not infallible.

Kaiser Wilhelm II, Generalfeldmarschall von Hindenburg and General von Ludendorff. (IWM, Q23746)

The left flank of Heeresgruppe Rupprecht was defended by 17. Armee under the command of **General Otto von Below.** Below commanded I Reservekorps at the outbreak of the war and fought on the Eastern Front in 1914. He took over 8. Armee in November, which he led through the Courland Offensive in 1915. In October 1916 he was given his own army group in Macedonia, commanding German and Bulgarian forces before moving to the west in April 1917 to command 6. Armee at Lille. In September he moved to Italy, where he led the Austro-German 14. Armee's stunning success at Caporetto. Consequently, he was returned to the West in February 1918 to command 17. Armee on the northern flank of Operation *Michael*. However, facing the better prepared defences around Arras, he was unable to repeat his Italian achievements and failed to capture the city.

Below's forces south of the River Sensée consisted of II Bayerische Armeekorps commanded by **General Konrad Krafft von Delmensingen,** XVIII Armeekorps, commanded by

Kronprinz Rupprecht of Bavaria (front row, third from left), Commander Heeresgruppe Rupprecht, with his staff. (IWM, Q24005)

Generalleutnant Gunter von Etzel, and XIV Reservekorps, commanded by **Generalleutnant Curt von Morgen**. Delmensingen was Chief of Staff of 6. Armee in 1914 before taking over command of the Alpenkorps mountain division in 1915, leading it through Verdun and also in Serbia and Romania. In 1917 he was Chief of Staff to Heeresgruppe Württemburg before becoming Chief of Staff of 14. Armee in Italy for the Caporetto Offensive. He took over II Bayerische Armeekorps in April 1918. Etzel commanded 33. Infanterie-Division in 1914 before taking over 3. Kavallerie-Division on the Eastern Front. In 1918 he assumed command of XVII Armeekorps on the Avre and the Matz before moving to XVIII Armeekorps in August. Morgen commanded 3. Reserve-Infanterie-Division on the Eastern Front in 1914, then moved to I Reservekorps in November. He remained in the East until 1917, when his corps moved to the Western Front, fighting on the Avre and the Matz in 1918. In August 1918 he assumed command of XIV Reservekorps.

South of Cambrai were 2. Armee and 18. Armee of Heeresgruppe Boehn, commanded by **General Max von Boehn**. Boehn was brought out of retirement in 1914 and assumed command of IX Reservekorps on the Western Front, where he fought throughout 1915 as trench warfare became established. In 1916 his corps saw action at Verdun on the 'Giessler Height' and the Somme before he was promoted to command Army Detachment 'C'

General Otto von Below (right), Commander German 17. Armee. (IWM, Q23980)

on the Meuse in February 1917. In March he moved to 7. Armee in Champagne where he fought on the Chemin des Dames in May and at Malmaison in October. His army made significant gains around Reims during the Spring Offensive in May 1918 before he was appointed to command his own army group in August. Boehn was a highly experienced officer who celebrated his 50th year of military service in December 1917. He was an extremely effective tactical commander, winning the *Pour le Mérite* with Oak Leaves for his actions on the Somme and the Chemin des Dames.

General Max von Boehn, Commander Heeresgruppe von Boehn. (IWM, Q70778)

General **Adolph von Carlowitz** commanded 2. Armee. Carlowitz began the war as the Minister for War in the Kingdom of Saxony and took over XXVII Reservekorps on mobilization. However, he failed to cope with the stress of combat at Ypres and was relieved of his duties. He spent the first half of 1915 in command of 12. Reserve-Infanterie-Division before moving to the Eastern Front in August to lead III Reservekorps during the Lake Naroch Offensive. He returned to the west in August 1917 to command XIX Armeekorps, which he led with some success on the Lys in April 1918. In August he briefly took over the 9. Armee until it was dissolved in the aftermath of the battle of Épehy. A week later he replaced Marwitz in command of 2. Armee.

2. Armee consisted of 54. Generalkommando, commanded by **Generalleutnant Alfred von Larisch**; IV Reservekorps, commanded by **Generalleutnant Richard von Conta**; and 51. Generalkommando, commanded by **Generalleutnant Hans von Below**. Larisch commanded the 10., 81. and Garde-Ersatz Divisions between October 1914 and January 1918, seeing combat on the Meuse in 1914, on the Eastern Front in 1915, at Verdun in 1916 and at Riga in 1917. He took over 54. Generalkommando in January 1918 and fought at Soissons in May. Conta commanded 1. Infanterie-Division on the Eastern Front in 1914–15 and at Verdun in 1916. In August he took over IV Reservekorps in the Balkans before bringing it back to the west for the Spring Offensive in 1918. Below commanded Augusta-Garde-Grenadier-Regiment from the outbreak of the war until 1916, seeing combat in Belgium, Poland and eastern Russia. In October 1916 he assumed command of 89. Infanterie-Division in Romania, before returning to France in January 1917 to lead 238. Infanterie-Division at Arras, Ypres and the opening assault of the Spring Offensive. He assumed command of 51. Generalkommando in August 1918.

Defending the sector from St Quentin to the Oise was 18. Armee, commanded by **General Oskar von Hutier**. Hutier commanded 1. Garde-Infanterie-Division in the West in 1914, seeing action on the Marne. Between April 1915 and January 1917 he commanded XXI Armeekorps before moving east to take over 8. Armee in April. Here he gained a formidable reputation for the exploitation of infiltration tactics and surprise artillery bombardments, particularly at Riga in September. He returned to the West in December 1917 to assume command of 18. Armee for Operation *Michael*, where he shattered the British Fifth Army on the Somme.

I Bayerische Armeekorps was commanded by **Generalleutnant Nikolaus Ritter von Endres**. Endres commanded an infantry brigade until March 1915, when he was promoted to command 4. Bayerische-Infanterie-Division. He fought on the Somme in 1914, Loos in 1915, the Somme in 1916, Ypres in 1917 and Kemmel in 1918. He was promoted to command I Bayerische Armeekorps in June 1918. The other corps elements of 18. Armee were only peripherally engaged. They consisted of XXVI Reservekorps, commanded by **Generalleutnant Oskar Freiherr von Watter**, XVIII Reservekorps, commanded by **Generalleutnant Ludwig Sieger** and XIV Armeekorps commanded by **Generalleutnant Friedrich von Gontard**.

OPPOSING FORCES

THE BRITISH ARMY

By September 1918 the BEF was at the peak of its combat effectiveness, although competing national manpower demands promised to diminish its strength if the war went into 1919. Its combat performance was built on increasingly effective tactical and operational techniques, being lavishly supplied with state-of-the-art technology and being well led by experienced officers and NCOs. The principle of flanking attacks on enemy positions – by now well established for small units – was beginning to percolate up into higher formation tactical doctrine. It was included in the latest draft of the manual *SS 135 The Division in the Attack*, which was being circulated across the BEF for comment during August and its influence was already apparent in battle. Critically, the BEF's corps were beginning to manoeuvre more effectively with each other – such as the Canadian Corps and XVII Corps at the battle of the Drocourt–Quéant Line on 2 September – in order to crack the German line.

The presence of the Australian and Canadian corps was a key advantage. Both had retained the 12-battalion structure in their divisions when the remainder of the BEF had reduced to nine earlier in the year; both retained command of all their national divisions, and the Australians remained an all-volunteer force throughout. This strong and relatively stable structure enhanced *esprit de corps*, developed effective command and control systems and maximized their performance in battle. While the British formations perhaps lacked the élan of their Dominion colleagues in general, several were equally effective, such as IX and XVII corps, as they would show in the coming battle.

An Australian infantry platoon receiving a briefing. Only 18 men strong, from an establishment of 50, this picture illustrates the manpower problems that were biting deep into the BEF. This was offset by an increase in firepower, with two Lewis guns on display supplied with spare magazines carried by several platoon members. The haversack on each man's chest contained his respirator to protect against chemical attack. (IWM, E(AUS) 2790)

By 1918, each infantry platoon had enhanced firepower and assault techniques. The addition of Lewis guns and rifle grenades gave each platoon the firepower necessary to assault enemy positions independently, with both systems being used to cover the attack by riflemen and grenadiers. Where possible, these assaults were delivered from the flank or rear. There were usually four platoons to a company and four companies to a battalion. To increase the firepower available in support, 3in., 6in. and 9.45in. mortar batteries were available at brigade, division and corps levels respectively.

Like the infantry, the artillery had seen a rapid development of its capability. Better quality control of shell production and calibration of each gun enabled the batteries to fire much more accurately than previously. Combined with better maps and survey techniques, these improvements enabled the gunners to hit targets without the need to range their shots. Co-operation with the infantry was enhanced by the development of 'neutralizing fire' to augment the traditional 'destructive' bombardment techniques, in order to cover the approach of the assault troops until they were within metres of the objectives. Each division had two field artillery brigades, each consisting of three batteries equipped with 18-pdr guns and one battery equipped with 4.5in. howitzers. Additional field artillery brigades and heavy artillery brigades equipped with 60-pdr, 6in., 8in., 9.2in., 12in., 14in. and 15in. guns and howitzers were available at corps and army level. The increase in quantity and quality of heavy artillery was fundamental to the improvement in the BEF's effectiveness. In July 1916 it had 658 heavy artillery pieces in France. In July 1917 it had 1,744, and by September 1918 it had 2,206 on charge. When concentrated around the chosen assault sectors, these weapons gave the BEF the ability to dominate the German artillery ranged against them. Finally, the first British consignment of mustard gas ammunition had arrived to provide 32,000 rounds for Fourth Army's 18-pdr and 6in. howitzers.

Despite its limited success on the Western Front since 1914, the cavalry had retained and developed its capability as the exploitation arm. In September 1918 the Cavalry Corps underwent a fundamental reorganization as it prepared for the assault on the Hindenburg Line. The 2nd Cavalry Division was broken up, with the 3rd, 4th and 5th Cavalry Brigades attached to First, Third and Fourth Armies respectively, to provide an exploitation force under direct control of the front-line commanders for more timely employment. To replace them, the corps had been augmented with a 'motorized' infantry brigade in buses, two motor machine gun battalions, an infantry cyclist battalion and an armoured car battalion. The two remaining divisions each consisted of three brigades, each of three regiments. Although traditional cavalry weapons were retained, the troopers were equipped with the same Lee Enfield rifles as their infantry counterparts and fought with firepower as much as cold steel. In support of the corps was a mounted artillery brigade. Once the German front line had been penetrated, it was intended that this all-arms formation would strike deep into the rear and seize key railway communication centres.

Shells being manufactured in the National Shell Filling Factory in Birtley, County Durham. By late 1918, the full weight of British and Imperial industry was supporting the war effort. Between noon on 28 September and noon on 29 September, the BEF fired 943,847 rounds of artillery ammunition. It was the maximum expenditure in one day of the entire war. (IWM, Q27737)

The operation to breach the Hindenburg Line would rely greatly on the performance of the Royal Engineers, particularly in crossing the Canal du Nord and the St Quentin Canal. Each division possessed three field companies to support its brigades. A further field company per division was available for tasks in the army or corps areas. Basic 'stock span' steel bridging had been introduced early in the war, and in 1917, Hopkins and Inglis heavy bridges were brought into service, which would be critical for the task ahead.

British cavalry crossing the river Canche during the experimental exercise run on 17 September 1918. Haig's intent was to develop a mobile force capable of exploiting any opportunity to move though a break in the German defences and seize objectives in their rear areas. (IWM, Q9314)

The Tank Corps would also be critical in assisting the Hindenburg Line assault, using its vehicles to breach wire obstacles and bring heavier firepower to bear on German strongpoints. The Mk. V tank was the mainstay of the force, armed with 6-pdr cannon or machine guns and driven by a 150hp engine at 4.6mph. Newer vehicles, such as the 'Whippet' light tank and a variety of armoured cars, had been developed to more rapidly exploit opportunities to disrupt the German defensive system in greater depth. Some of the Mk. V tanks had also been 'stretched' to provide space to carry infantry machine-gun crews to deeper objectives. All of the vehicles, however, were uncomfortable for their crews, required extensive maintenance and lacked endurance on the battlefield.

Air support was provided by the newly formed Royal Air Force. Each army was supported permanently by an RAF brigade, each consisting of a corps wing, an army wing and a balloon wing. Each corps wing assisted the balloon wing in controlling artillery fire close to the front line and maintaining contact with the foremost troops in battle. The army wings consisted of bomber, fighter and fighter-reconnaissance squadrons to take the aerial battle beyond the front lines, to protect the corps wing and to deny German aircraft the opportunity to operate over British lines. In addition to each army-affiliated RAF Brigade, IX Brigade, consisting of two army wings and a night operations wing, was tasked by GHQ to whichever army required more concentrated aerial support.

Attached to Fourth Army was II (US) Corps. This corps had been in France since July 1918, undertaking a period of training and deployments with the BEF at Ypres to develop its combat experience. While most American units similarly familiarized with Western Front combat had since been concentrated into the American First Army under Pershing on the Meuse, II (US) Corps had been retained in the BEF to offset British manpower shortages. II (US) Corps consisted of 27th and 30th Infantry Divisions, each of which was substantially larger than their BEF counterparts, being established for 28,000 men. Each division was made up of two brigades, each containing two regiments of three infantry battalions and supporting units. Although one American field artillery battalion had been retained, the remainder was provided by the Australian Corps. While strong in number and possessing high morale, II (US) Corps was critically weak in combat experience in comparison to the BEF. This was exacerbated by Pershing's decision to remove junior officers for centralized American training, although given the pace and scale of American engagement in the war he had little alternative.

Troops of 27th (US) Division training for combat alongside tanks. (IWM, Q57694)

Morale in the BEF was generally good following the successful summer operations, although the prospect of assaulting the Hindenburg Line with its formidable reputation was somewhat daunting. Fatigue was also a concern, as even elite units such as the Australians were beginning to show the strain of extended combat on the Western Front. They were, however, well trained, well equipped and confident in their leaders and themselves.

THE FRENCH ARMY

Although the French Army of 1918 was tactically effective, the necessity to conserve manpower tempered its approach to battle. It also developed tactical techniques that maximized the used the firepower from artillery and machine guns to spare its infantry, with envelopment and flank attack being the preferred manoeuvre. Each infantry division contained three infantry regiments, each of three battalions of 700 men. Rifle platoons had rifle, bombing and light machine-gun squads. Each battalion had a machine-gun company and was equipped with 37mm infantry cannon alongside 45mm and 60mm mortars. The French units included a large number of troops from the French colonies. *Zouaves* were recruited from Frenchmen living overseas and had a tough fighting reputation, while the *tirailleurs* were recruited from the indigenous colonial populations.

The artillery increased from 20 per cent of the army in 1914 to 38 per cent by 1918. The outstanding 75mm field gun from the pre-war divisions had been augmented with 105mm, 120mm and 155mm howitzers. These were supported in turn by heavier pieces, including the 220mm and 370mm weapons assigned to Debeney's 1re Armee for the coming battle.

Unlike the British, the French air arm had not become a separate service. Each army and corps had a number of fighter, reconnaissance and bomber squadrons. A proportion of the air service *escadrilles* had been grouped into a powerful Division Aérienne, but this was assigned to the Meuse-Argonne operation.

THE GERMAN ARMY

The German Army was in serious difficulties in September 1918. 17., 2. and 18. Armees had formed the spearhead of Operation *Michael* and received little respite in the subsequent months as the cream of their divisions continually shuffled from Flanders to Champagne to support the other assaults. The remainder spent extended periods in the line, exposed to the depredations of aggressive BEF patrolling, in particular from the Australians. Perhaps more concerning was that fact that their defensive positions seemed increasingly difficult to retain. Even when successful defensive engagements had been fought, prisoners had been lost in unprecedented numbers. This suggested that while the German Army remained a dangerous tactical adversary, morale was increasingly fragile. In short, it was rapidly approaching the point beyond which it could no longer continue the war.

German defence was still based on the doctrine disseminated at the end of 1917. A forward zone approximately 500–1,000m deep consisted of small outposts to hold off enemy patrols and to disrupt small-scale attacks. Behind this was the battle zone approximately 2,500m deep. The forward edge was normally the main line of resistance and was held by the front-line battalions, with support and reserve units further back in each regimental sector. Behind the front-line divisions were the *Eingrief* divisions, tasked to move forwards when required to block penetrations and re-establish the original front line if possible. However, the understrength front-line divisions now lacked the manpower to adequately defend their sectors to the width or depth required. This resulted in too great a proportion of their infantry being pulled into the forward positions, where they remained under threat from the Allied artillery fire or flanking infantry attacks. Furthermore, those left to the rear were generally too weak to mount successful counter-attacks when required.

The core of the German Army was the infantry division, consisting of three infantry regiments, each of three battalions, an artillery command and supporting troops. Although each division was established at 12,500 men,

Dismounted German cavalry launch a counter-attack. Due to infantry manpower shortages in 1918, 27 German cavalry regiments were dismounted and reorganized into three *Kavallerie-Schützen-Divisons* (5., 6. and 7.). Each *Kavallerie-Schützen-Division* consisted of nine cavalry regiments grouped into three *Kavallerie-Schützen-Kommandos*, each the equivalent of an *Infanterie-Regiment*. Each had a *Feld-Artillerie-Regiment*, and 7. also had a *Füss-Artillerie-Regiment*. (IWM, Q55024)

most were considerably below this strength by September 1918. In August, infantry battalion manning was reduced from 800 to 750 men, with those under 650 reorganized into three rifle companies instead of four. By the end of September, battalions were averaging 540 men strong. Regiments with battalions of fewer than 400 men were reorganized into two battalions. Each battalion had a machine-gun company with 12 guns, augmented by six light machine guns in each rifle company. A light mortar company with six 76mm mortars supported the riflemen and machine-gunners in each strongpoint to provide a deep, fire-swept zone in which to defeat the Allied assaults. The line infantry formations were augmented in 1917 and 1918 by *Jäger* and cavalry units re-grouped into divisional-sized formations and retrained for dismounted combat.

The artillery command consisted of three battalions, each of two batteries equipped with 77mm field guns and one battery of 105mm light howitzers, and a heavy *füß* artillery battalion, with two batteries of 150mm howitzers and one battery of 100mm guns. The divisional artillery was supported by batteries of heavier calibre guns and howitzers under corps and army HQ control. The British combination of armour and surprise artillery barrages since the battle of Amiens posed a significant tactical dilemma to the Germans. Whereas previous defensive doctrine envisaged the field guns being concentrated behind the main line of resistance for their own protection, an increasing proportion were now pulled into the foremost positions to provide close defence and anti-tank support. The remainder of the guns, however, were deployed further away in order to escape capture from the deeper British penetrations. These somewhat contradictory actions exposed the forward guns to capture in the initial assault, while those deployed in depth found it much more difficult to coordinate effective fire support to the front line. The disruption of the German defensive firepower in this manner was a critical factor in the late summer and autumn battles of 1918.

The Luftstreitkräfte lacked the numbers of the Allied air forces, but possessed exceptional aircraft, and in September 1918, exacted a heavy toll during bitter combat. The fighters of the *Jagdstaffeln* (Jastas) and the ground attack aircraft of the *Schlactstaffeln* (Schlastas) were concentrated on the most active fronts, with only a smaller proportion permanently assigned to specific locations. The Jastas were increasingly equipped with the excellent Fokker DVII, while the Schlastas mainly flew the Halberstadt CLII and CLIV aircraft, specializing in low-level attack missions. Reconnaissance and artillery cooperation tasks were conducted by *Fliegerabteilung* (FA) and *Fliegerabteilung (Artillerie)* FA(A) units. During operations, the Jastas were normally controlled at army level to assist concentration of force, while control of the Schlastas, FAs and FA(A)s was normally devolved to corps level to ensure better integration with the ground battle.

German field gun deployed in the anti-tank role in forward positions. (IWM, E(AUS) 3411)

ORDERS OF BATTLE

BRITISH ARMY, 27 SEPTEMBER 1918

FIRST ARMY – GEN. SIR HENRY HORNE

VIII Corps – Lt. Gen. Sir Aylmer Hunter-Weston
XXII Corps – Lt. Gen. Sir Alexander Godley
51st Division – Maj. Gen. Carter-Campbell
    173rd Brigade
    174th Brigade
    175th Brigade
56th Division – Maj. Gen. Hull
    167th Brigade
    168th Brigade
    169th Brigade
Canadian Corps – Lt. Gen. Sir Arthur Currie
1st Canadian Division – Maj. Gen. Macdonell
    1st Canadian Brigade
    2nd Canadian Brigade
    3rd Canadian Brigade
2nd Canadian Division – Maj. Gen. Burstall
    4th Canadian Brigade
    5th Canadian Brigade
    6th Canadian Brigade
3rd Canadian Division – Maj. Gen. Loomis
    7th Canadian Brigade
    8th Canadian Brigade
    9th Canadian Brigade
4th Canadian Division – Maj. Gen. Watson
    10th Canadian Brigade
    11th Canadian Brigade
    12th Canadian Brigade
11th Division – Brig. Gen. de l'E Winter
    32nd Brigade
    33rd Brigade
    Brutinel's Brigade

Army Troops
3rd Cavalry Brigade
7th Tank Battalion

Royal Air Force
I Brigade RAF

THIRD ARMY – GEN. HON. SIR JULIAN BYNG

XVII Corps – Lt. Gen. Sir Charles Fergusson Bt
52nd Division – Maj. Gen. Marshall
    155th Brigade
    156th Brigade
    157th Brigade
57th Division – Maj. Gen. Barnes
    170th Brigade
    171st Brigade
    172nd Brigade
63rd Division – Maj. Gen. Blacklock
    188th Brigade
    189th Brigade
    190th Brigade
VI Corps – Lt. Gen. Sir Aylmer Haldane
Guards Division – Maj. Gen. Matheson
    1st Guards Brigade
    2nd Guards Brigade
    3rd Guards Brigade
2nd Division – Maj. Gen. Pereira
    5th Brigade
    6th Brigade
    99th Brigade
3rd Division – Maj. Gen. Deverell
    8th Brigade

    9th Brigade
    76th Brigade
62nd Division – Maj. Gen. Whigham
    185th Brigade
    186th Brigade
    187th Brigade
IV Corps – Lt. Gen. Sir Montague Harper
5th Division – Maj. Gen. Ponsonby
    13th Brigade
    15th Brigade
    95th Brigade
37th Division – Maj. Gen. Bruce Williams
    63rd Brigade
    111th Brigade
    112th Brigade
42nd Division – Maj. Gen. Solly-Flood
    125th Brigade
    126th Brigade
    127th Brigade
New Zealand Division – Maj. Gen. Russell
    1st New Zealand Brigade
    2nd New Zealand Brigade
    3rd New Zealand Brigade
V Corps – Lt. Gen. Sir Cameron Shute
17th Division – Maj. Gen. Robertson
    50th Brigade
    51st Brigade
    52nd Brigade
21st Division – Maj. Gen. Campbell
    62nd Brigade
    64th Brigade
    110th Brigade
33rd Division – Maj. Gen. Pinney
    19th Brigade
    98th Brigade
    100th Brigade
38th Division – Maj. Gen. Cubitt
    113th Brigade
    114th Brigade
    155th Brigade

Army Troops
4th Cavalry Brigade
11th Tank Battalion
12th Tank Battalion
15th Tank Battalion

Royal Air Force
III Brigade RAF

FOURTH ARMY – GEN. SIR HENRY RAWLINSON BT

III Corps – Lt. Gen. Sir Richard Butler
12th Division – Maj. Gen. Higginson
    35th Brigade
    36th Brigade
    37th Brigade
18th Division – Maj. Gen. Lee
    53rd Brigade
    54th Brigade
    55th Brigade
58th Division – Maj. Gen. Ramsey
    173rd Brigade
    174th Brigade
    175th Brigade
74th Division – Maj. Gen. Girdwood
    229th Brigade
    230th Brigade
    231st Brigade

XIII Corps – Lt. Gen. Sir Thomas Morland
25th Division – Maj. Gen. Charles
    7th Brigade
    74th Brigade
    75th Brigade
50th Division – Maj. Gen. Jackson
    149th Brigade
    150th Brigade
    151st Brigade
66th Division – Maj. Gen. Bethell
    198th Brigade
    199th Brigade
    South African Brigade
Australian Corps – Lt. Gen. Sir John Monash
2nd Australian Division – Maj. Gen. Rosenthal
    5th Australian Brigade
    6th Australian Brigade
    7th Australian Brigade
3rd Australian Division – Maj. Gen. Gellibrand
    9th Australian Brigade
    10th Australian Brigade
    11th Australian Brigade
5th Australian Division – Maj. Gen. Talbot Hobbs
    8th Australian Brigade
    14th Australian Brigade
    15th Australian Brigade
27th American Division – Maj. Gen. O'Ryan
    105th Infantry Regiment
    106th Infantry Regiment
    107th Infantry Regiment
    108th Infantry Regiment
30th American Division – Maj. Gen. Lewis
    117th Infantry Regiment
    118th Infantry Regiment
    119th Infantry Regiment
    120th Infantry Regiment
IX Corps – Lt. Gen. Sir Walter Braithwaite
1st Division – Maj. Gen. Strickland
    1st Brigade
    2nd Brigade
    3rd Brigade
6th Division – Maj. Gen. Marden
    16th Brigade
    18th Brigade
    71st Brigade
32nd Division – Maj. Gen. Lambert
    14th Brigade
    96th Brigade
    97th Brigade
46th Division – Maj. Gen. Boyd
    136th Brigade
    137th Brigade
    138th Brigade

Army Troops
5th Cavalry Brigade
1st Tank Battalion – Mk. V
3rd Tank Battalion – Whippet
4th Tank Battalion – Mk. V
5th Tank Battalion – Mk. V
6th Tank Battalion – Whippet
8th Tank Battalion – Mk. V
13th Tank Battalion – Mk. V
16th Tank Battalion – Mk. V*
301st (US) Tank Battalion – Mk. V
17th Armoured Car Battalion

Royal Air Force
V Brigade RAF

GHQ TROOPS

Cavalry Corps – Lt. Gen. Sir Charles Kavanagh
1st Cavalry Division – Maj. Gen. Mullens

    1st Cavalry Brigade
    2nd Cavalry Brigade
    9th Cavalry Brigade
3rd Cavalry Division – Maj. Gen. Harman
    6th Cavalry Brigade
    7th Cavalry Brigade
    Canadian Cavalry Brigade
4th Guards Brigade
Household Cavalry Machine Gun Brigade

Royal Air Force
IX Brigade RAF

FRENCH ARMY, 27 SEPTEMBER 1918

1RE ARMÉE – GÉN. EUGÈNE DEBENEY

15e Corps d'Armée – Gén. de Riols de Fonclare
46e Division – Gén. Gratier
    1re GBC
    2e GBC
    3e GBC
47e Division – Gén. Dillemann
    4e GBC
    5e GBC
    6e GBC
126e Division – Gén. Mathieu
    55e RI
    112e RI
    173e RI
36e Corps d'Armée – Gén. Nollet
133e Division – Gén. Valentin
    321e RI
    401e RI
    15e GBC
166e Division – Gén. Cabaud
    171e RI
    294e RI
    19e BCP
    26e BCP
31e Corps d'Armée – Gén. Toulorge
56e Division – Gén. Demetz
    106e RI
    132e RI
    10e GBC
152e Division – Gén. Andrieu
    11e RI
    125e RI
    135e RI
169e Division – Gén. Serat Almeras Latour
    13e RI
    29e RI
    39e RI
8e Corps d'Armée – Gén. Hély d'Oissel
37e Division – Gén. Simon
    2e RZ
    2e RT
    3e RZ
    3e RT
67e Division – Gén. Bousquier
    283e RI
    288e RI
    369e RI
123e Division – Gén. de Saint-Just
    6e RI
    12e RI
    411e RI
58e Division – Gén. Priou
    412e RI
    6e RT
    11e RT
60e Division – Gén. Jacquemot
    202e RI

225e RI
248e RI

ARMY TROOPS

15e Division – Gén. Arbanève
    10e RI
    56e RI
    134e RI
34e Division – Gén. Savatier
    59e RI
    83e RI
    88e RI
64e Division – Gén. Colin
    269e RI
    331e RI
    340e RI
70e Division – Gén. Tantôt
    226e RI
    360e RI
    17e GBC

Key to abbreviations
BCP – Battalions chasseurs à pied
GBC – Groupe des battalions chasseurs
RI – Régiment d'infanterie
RT – Régiment de tirailleurs
RZ – Régiment de zouaves

GERMAN ARMY, 27 SEPTEMBER 1918

17. ARMEE – GEN. OTTO VON BELOW

I Bayerische Reserve Armeekorps – Gen. Karl Ritter von Faßbender
111. Infanterie-Division – GenMaj. von Busse
    FüsR 73
    IR 76
    IR 164
15. Reserve-Division – GenMaj. Hucke
    RIR 17
    RIR 25
    RIR 69
234. Infanterie-Division – GenMaj. von Stumpff
    IR 451
    IR 452
    IR 453
48. Reserve-Division – GenMaj. von Hippel
    RIR 221
    RIR 222
    RIR 223
220. Infanterie-Division – GenMaj. von Bassewitz
    RIR 55
    RIR 90
    IR 190

II Bayerische Armeekorps – Gen. Konrad Krafft von Delmensingen
214. Infanterie-Division – GenMaj. Maercker
    IR 50
    IR 343
    IR 358
35. Infanterie-Division – GenMaj. Wohlgenuth
    IR 61
    IR 141
    IR 176
58. (Sächs) Infanterie-Division – GenMaj. Graf von Eckstaedt
    RIR 103
    IR 106
    IR 107
22. Infanterie-Division – GenMaj. Neubaur
    IR 82
    IR 83
    IR 167

XVIII Armeekorps – GenLt. Günter von Etzel
12. Infanterie-Division – GenMaj. von Funcke

    IR 23
    IR 62
    IR 63
187. Infanterie-Division – GenMaj. von Langermann und Erlenkamp
    IR 187
    IR 188
    IR 189
7. Kavallerie-Schützen-Division – GenMaj. von Heuduck
    KSK 28
    KSK 30
    KSK 41
1. Garde-Reserve-Division – GenMaj. Tiede
    GRR 1
    GRR 2
    IR 64
207. Infanterie-Division – GenMaj. Mattiaß
    IR 98
    IR 208
    IR 209

XIV Reservekorps – GenLt. Curt von Morgen
49. Reserve-Division – GenMaj. von Uechtritz und Steinkirch
    RIR 225
    RIR 226
    RIR 228
20. Infanterie-Division – GenMaj. Zwenger
    IR 77
    IR 79
    IR 92
6. Infanterie-Division – GenMaj. von Mutius
    IR 24
    IR 64
    IR 396
113. Infanterie-Division – GenMaj. von Passow
    RIR 32
    Füs R 36
    IR 66
3. Marine-Division – GenMaj. Graf von Moltke
    MIR 1
    MIR 2
    MIR 3
18. Reserve-Division – GenMaj. von Wrisberg
    RIR 31
    RIR 84
    RIR 86

2. ARMEE – GEN. ADOLPH VON CARLOWITZ

54. Generalkommando – GenLt. Alfred von Larisch
Jäger Division – GenMaj. von Dassel
    JägR 11
    JägR 12
    JägR 13
21. Reserve-Division – GenMaj. Briese
    RIR 80
    RIR 87
    RIR 88
30. Infanterie-Division – GenMaj. Riebensahm
    IR 99
    IR 105
    IR 143
201. Infanterie-Division – GenMaj. Bachelin
    IR 401
    IR 402
    IR 403

IV Reservekorps – GenLt. Richard von Conta
8. Infanterie-Division – GenMaj. Hamann
    IR 72
    IR 93
    IR 153
54. Infanterie-Division – GenMaj. Kabisch
    RIR 27
    IR 84
    RIR 90
121. Infanterie-Division – GenMaj. Breßler

RIR 7
RIR 56
IR 60
2. Garde-Division – GenMaj. von Friedeburg
    Kaiser Alexander GGrenR
    Kaiser Franz GGrenR
    Königin Augusta GGrenR

51. Generalkommando – GenLt. Hans von Below
185. Infanterie-Division – GenMaj. von Horn
    RIR 28
    IR 65
    IR 161
75. Reserve-Division – GenMaj. von Eisenhardt-Rothe
    RIR 249
    RIR 250
    RIR 251
2. Infanterie-Division – GenMaj. von Dommes
    GrenR 4
    FüsR 33
    IR 44
21. Infanterie-Division – GenMaj. von Wahlen-Jürgaß
    FüsR 80
    IR 81
    IR 87

18. ARMEE – GEN. OSKAR VON HUTIER

I Bayerische Armeekorps – GenLt. von Endres
79. Reserve-Division – GenMaj. Landauer
    RIR 261
    RIR 262
    RIR 263
197. Infanterie-Division – GenMaj. von Alt-Stutterheim
    RIR 273
    SächsJägR 7
    ErzR 28
82. Reserve-Division – GenMaj. von Lorne de St Ange
    RIR 270
    RIR 271
    RIR 272
221. Infanterie-Division – GenMaj. von der Chevallerie
    IR 41
    RIR 60
    IR 45
11. Infanterie-Division – GenMaj. Freiherr Schmidt von Schmidtseck
    GrenR 10
    FüsR 38
    IR 51
25. Reserve-Division – GenMaj. Mattiaß
    RIR 83
    RIR 118
    IR 168
34. Infanterie-Division – GenMaj. Teetzmann
    IR 30
    IR 67
    IR 145
206. Infanterie-Division – GenMaj. von Etzel
    IR 359
    IR 394
    RErzR 4

XXVI Reservekorps – GenLt. Freiherr von Watter
22. Reserve-Division – GenMaj. Schubert
    RIR 71
    RIR 82
    RIR 94
6. Bayerische-Infanterie-Division – GenMaj. Ritter von Rauchenberger
    BayIR 6
    BayIR 10
    Bay IR 13
231. Infanterie-Division – GenMaj. von Dewitz
    IR 442
    IR 443
    IR 444

208. Infanterie-Division – GenMaj. von Groddeck
    IR 25
    IR 185
    RIR 65
XVIII Reservekorps – GenLt. Sieger
241. (Sächs) Infanterie-Division – GenMaj. Fortmüller
    IR 472
    IR 473
    IR 474
84. Infanterie-Division – GenMaj. Leu
    IR 335
    IR 336
    IR 423
XIV Armeekorps – GenLt. von Gontard
237. Infanterie-Division – GenMaj. von Jacobi
    IR 460
    IR 461
    IR 462
24. (Sächs) Infanterie-Division – GenMaj. Hammer
    IR 133
    IR 139
    IR 179
105. Infanterie-Division – GenMaj. Schaer
    IR 21
    IR 129
    IR 400

OHL RESERVES

26. (Württemburgische) Reserve-Division – GenMaj. von Fritsch (Caudry)
    RIR 119
    RIR 121
    IR 180
38. Infanterie-Division – GenMaj. Schultheis (Solesmes)
    IR 94
    IR 95
    IR 96
5. Bayerische-Infanterie-Division – GenMaj. von Clauß (Le Cateau)
    Bay IR 7
    Bay IR 19
    Bay IR 21
119. Infanterie-Division – GenMaj. Hagenberg (Barzy)
    IR 46
    RIR 46
    IR 58
1. Reserve-Division – GenMaj. von Waldersee (Le Nouvion)
    RIR 1
    RIR 3
    RIR 59
232. Infanterie-Division – GenMaj. von Dewitz (Guise)
    FüsR 36
    IR 65
    RIR 32
3. Landwehr Division – GenMaj. Zierold (Guise)
    LIR 6
    LIR 7
    LIR 46

Key to abbreviations
Bay – Bayerische
FüsR – Füsilier-Regiment
GRR – Garde-Reserve-Regiment
GrenR – Grenadier-Regiment
GGrenR – Garde-Grenadier-Regiment
IR – Infanterie-Regiment
JägR – Jäger-Regiment
KSK – Kavallerie-Schützen-Kommando
LIR – Landwehr-Infanterie-Regiment
MIR – Marine-Infanterie-Regiment
RErzR – Reserve-Ersatz-Regiment
RIR – Reserve-Infanterie Regiment
Sächs – Sächsische

OPPOSING PLANS

ALLIED PLANS

Although Foch's strategy had roots that could be traced back to December 1914, the operational and tactical plans of 1918 were fundamentally changed. The offensives of 1915–17 aimed to breach multiple defensive lines in one bound and consequently took significant amounts of time to plan in great detail. These intricate schemes often failed to allow for the uncertainties of combat, demanded too much from their inexperienced command teams and often chafed against competing national priorities. By late 1918, however, the Allied commanders were working with each other in a far more cooperative manner, with plans better attenuated to the capabilities of their troops, and which developed detail incrementally as the campaign situation developed.

As the first phase of Foch's strategic directive neared completion, the operational planning to breach the Hindenburg Line increased in tempo. Noting Pershing's plan for an advance towards Metz, Haig wrote to Foch on 27 August, proposing that after the forthcoming American operation to reduce the St Mihiel salient, the AEF's exploitation be shifted towards Mézières instead of Metz, to improve the mutual support between the Allied armies in the subsequent advances. This suggestion coincided with Foch's developing plan to seize the key strategic railway linking Germany with the central and western parts of the front. But he also wanted to commence the exploitation as quickly as possible lest the Germans gain time to reorganize. The proposed change did not go down well with Pershing, who looked towards the St Mihiel–Metz operations as being the signal event of the AEF's arrival in the war. However, after a series of fractious meetings and telegrams, Pershing agreed to the new plan with the proviso that the American contribution to the Mézières operation would be as an independent army alongside the French 4e Armée rather than as part of a larger French force. Consequently, on 3 September Foch issued a further directive, combining the Franco-US attack towards Mézières with the British thrusts towards Cambrai–St Quentin.

Foch further developed the scope of his offensive on 9 September when he added an attack by the British, French and Belgian forces in the Groupe d'Armées de Flandres (GAF) to the original scheme. This was followed on 16 and 19 September by the addition of attacks by the French 5e and 10e Armées across the Aisne and Chemin des Dames to cover the left flank of the assault towards Mézières. Only the timing of each Allied thrust remained

Haig's plan

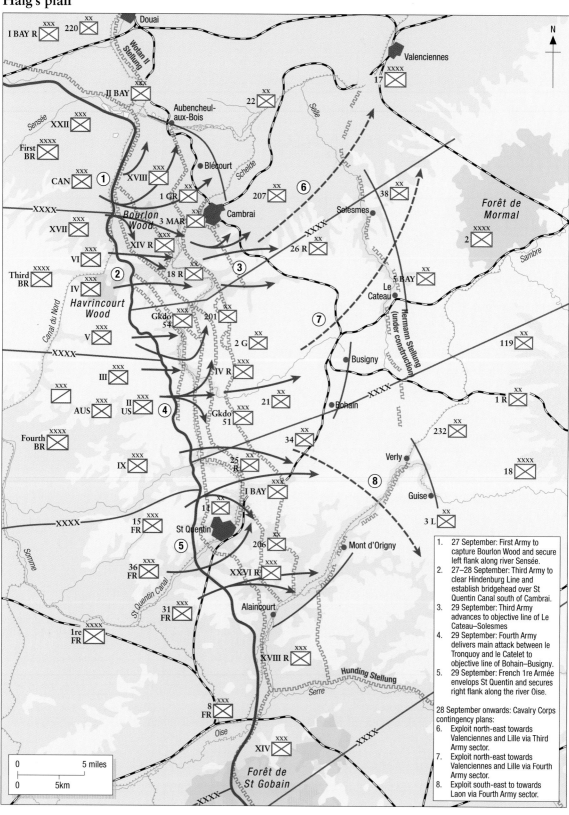

1. 27 September: First Army to capture Bourlon Wood and secure left flank along river Sensée.
2. 27–28 September: Third Army to clear Hindenburg Line and establish bridgehead over St Quentin Canal south of Cambrai.
3. 29 September: Third Army advances to objective line of Le Cateau–Solesmes
4. 29 September: Fourth Army delivers main attack between le Tronquoy and le Catelet to objective line of Bohain–Busigny.
5. 29 September: French 1re Armée envelops St Quentin and secures right flank along the river Oise.

28 September onwards: Cavalry Corps contingency plans:
6. Exploit north-east towards Valenciennes and Lille via Third Army sector.
7. Exploit north-east towards Valenciennes and Lille via Fourth Army sector.
8. Exploit south-east to towards Laon via Fourth Army sector.

to be confirmed. While Foch was concerned that they would need to be sequenced to offset logistic constraints, Haig was equally worried about the need to draw away the German forces most heavily concentrated on the front he was to attack. After further deliberation, on 23 September Foch directed that what was now termed the General Offensive would commence three days later, with each operation being launched at one-day intervals. The Franco-US assault towards Mézières was to be launched first on 26 September, with the British assault towards Cambrai commencing the following day. The Flanders operation was to be launched next on 28 September, with the culminating British attack on the main Hindenburg Line defences north of St Quentin taking place on 29 September. The subsidiary attacks by the French 10e and 5e Armées were to be launched on 27 and 30 September respectively.

This ambitious plan promised to stretch Ludendorff's forces to the limit. The German Army had 190 divisions on the Western Front – 125 in the front line and 65 in reserve – but in response to the Allied campaign's development during August and September, too many were increasingly threatened with isolation east of the Meuse. Whereas Armee Abteilung 'C' and Heeresgruppe Württemburg consisted of 25 front-line and 4 reserve divisions at the end of August, by 21 September they had been reinforced with a further six front-line and 18 reserve divisions to block any further American advance towards Metz and the east. This misconception was deliberately reinforced by Foch's visit to Nancy and Belfort between 19 and 22 September. As the German reserves shuffled to the east, 17., 2. and 18. Armees reduced their combined strength by 18 divisions. In this respect, Haig's aim to draw off German forces facing the BEF was already achieved, as the St Mihiel attack had become a feint for the General Offensive.

In addition to his influential role in the development of the strategic and higher operational plans of the Allied armies, Haig was also deeply involved in orchestrating the tactical plans for the First, Third and Fourth Armies' attacks. On 8 September, Haig asked his Army Commanders – Generals Horne, Byng and Rawlinson – for their opinions on the assault on the Hindenburg Line. All three agreed that while they should attack quickly

German transport withdrawing across the St Quentin Canal at Bellenglise in September 1918. Each *Infanterie-Regiment* had 233 horses and 72 wagons to transport its equipment. Despite the advent of the motor vehicle, all armies on the Western Front depended on horsepower for transport. That this team is pulling two wagons highlights the acute shortage of draft animals in the German Army by this stage of the war. (IWM, Q60476)

to prevent the Germans reorganizing, due to the complexity and depth of the Hindenburg Line, the sequencing of discrete, limited scale operations would be required to disrupt the system without exposing their own troops to German counter-attacks. With Haig's consent, on 11 September Third Army seized the fortified village of Moeuvres overlooking the Canal du Nord to secure their grip on the west bank and cover right flank of the Canadians to their north. The following day it secured the Advanced Hindenburg Line around the key village of Havrincourt. Further south, on 18 September, Fourth Army did the same between Hargicourt and Pontruet at the battle of Épehy. The conditions were now set for Horne and Byng to attack the Main Hindenburg Line west of Cambrai and Rawlinson to do likewise over the St Quentin Canal.

Horne and Byng began their planning for the main assault on 15 September. Horne delegated the task of crossing the Canal du Nord to Lieutenant-General Currie's Canadian Corps. Currie's ambitious plan envisaged two divisions blasting their way through on a 2,500-yard front north of Mouevres. Thereafter, two further divisions were to join the assault as it fanned out to the north and east to envelop the heights around Bourlon Wood. Crossings over the Schelde Canal north of Cambrai were to be attempted if possible thereafter. In an attempt to impose an element of deception into the plan, Currie forbade daylight movement in forward areas, while Godley's XXII Corps was to conduct operations to simulate an attack across the whole front south of the Sensée. In Third Army's sector, Byng's problems were more complex. Notwithstanding that the Hindenburg Line ran obliquely away from his right wing, the fact that Fourth Army's assault was scheduled two days later than First Army's, meant that he had to maintain contact with the advancing First Army on his left and the relatively static Fourth Army on his right. He therefore directed XVII Corps to keep up with the Canadians on the left, while VI and IV Corps echeloned back to the right to where V Corps was broadly holding its position. In conjunction with the Canadians, XVII Corps was to cross the Canal du Nord on a narrow front and then fan out to the east and south before closing up to the St Quentin Canal in the vicinity of Rumilly. Although the Canadians were left in relative peace to conduct their preparations, XVII Corps was not so lucky. For ten days prior to the assault, they had to fight off bitter counter-attacks from XVIII Armeekorps attempting to recapture Moeuvres.

In the south, Rawlinson gave the main task to Lieutenant-General Monash's Australian Corps who, together with Major-General Read's II (US) Corps, were to breach the Hindenburg Line over the Bellicourt Tunnel. Eschewing the prospect of a difficult assault over the canal as it passed through its deep cuttings, Monash ordered the Americans to seize the Main Hindenburg Line between Bellicourt and Le Catelet before fanning out to the north and south. The Australians would then pass

Australian infantry digging in during the battle of Épehy on 18 September 1918. In the background can be seen the effects of the smokescreens fired by the artillery to blind the German defence, the machine-gunners in particular. (IWM, E(AUS) 3248)

through them and capture the Hindenburg Support and Reserve positions. Should this be successful, the 17th Armoured Car Battalion and the 6th Tank Battalion were to pass through the Australian infantry and conduct a deep raid towards the German communications hub at Busigny and Le Cateau. III Corps was to link the Australians with Third Army to the north. Rawlinson accepted the plan on 19 September with a significant alteration. He included Lieutenant-General Braithwaite's proposal that IX Corps would assault across the canal at Bellenglise simultaneously with the Australian and American attack. Throughout the week leading up to the main attack, both

The Hindenburg Line at Bellicourt looking east. The tunnel lies directly below the village, with the trenches of the Main Hindenburg Line covering the approaches from the west. In the background can be seen the villages of Nauroy, Estrées, Joncourt, Wiancourt, Ramicourt and, in the far distance, Montbrehain. (IWM, Q55630)

Lieutenant-General Butler's III Corps and IX Corps attempted to widen the breach in the Advanced Hindenburg Line with limited success. Such was Rawlinson's dissatisfaction with Butler, on 22 September Haig agreed to replace III Corps with Morland's XIII Corps, but rather than delay the attack to effect this change, Rawlinson instead ordered the Americans to seize the Advanced Hindenburg Line positions between Hargicourt and Tombois Farm as a preliminary to the main assault. III Corps was to provide flank security. The Cavalry Corps was retained under Haig's control but began to work up contingency plans to pass through either Third or Fourth Army and disrupt the German communications at either Valenciennes or Le Cateau.

In the air, IX Brigade RAF would begin the process of isolating the battlefield overnight 26/27 September by bombing the key railway stations of Denain, Busigny and Le Cateau before switching their attention to German airfields the following day. I Brigade RAF was to prevent German forces crossing the Sensée from the north, to drive down German observation balloons and provide close air support, while III Brigade RAF did the same on the St Quentin Canal south of Cambrai. As Fourth Army entered the fray on 29 September, V Brigade RAF was to fly in support, with priority targets being the destruction of enemy balloons, impeding German reserves approaching the battle, and neutralizing artillery batteries firing in the open.

From St Quentin to the Oise, Debeney's 1re Armée was ordered to support the right flank of the British, but remained under command of Fayolle's Groupe d'Armée Réserve (GAR). Fayolle's mission also required him to support the left flank of the Meuse-Argonne operation with Mangin's 10e Armée. Given that he was not the highest priority for resources across the French Army, on 20 September he instructed Debeney to operate with a strict economy of men and munitions to best husband those he had. Consequently, Debeney's plan, distributed on 25 September, was to envelop St Quentin from the north and south. He gave primacy to 15e Corps' assault, which was to assist 31e and 36e Corps' southern pincer by turning the Hindenburg Line north of St Quentin. However, as 15e Corps was not due to enter the line until the latter part of 29 September, this attack would be impossible to co-ordinate with Fourth Army's assault. In an attempt to resolve this contradiction, Debeney ordered 31e and 8e Corps to attack on 29 September between Urvillers and Cerizy to distract Hutier's 18. Armee.

GERMAN PLANS

While Foch and Haig were able to combine the efforts of their forces, Ludendorff was slowly losing his ability to do the same for the Germans. On 23 September, as the Allied focus shifted back to the west of the Meuse, OHL belatedly recognized that 22 of their reserve divisions were now poorly positioned in Alsace and Lorraine. In a desperate attempt to regain a more balanced deployment, orders were issued to move 12 divisions back across the Meuse to the west. However, the consequence of the increased number of divisions in Lorraine was a reduction in the reserves available to support 17., 2. and 18. Armees. Lacking the strength to defend the whole of their front in depth, Rupprecht and Boehn identified priority sectors in which to concentrate their reserve divisions. Four were deployed in 17. Armee covering the western approaches to Cambrai, three in 2. Armee covering the Bellicourt Tunnel and four in 18. Armee covering St Quentin. Critically, of 2. Armee's reserves, only one division was in the Bellenglise sector now targeted by Rawlinson, and this had detached one of its three regiments to IV Reservekorps at Bellicourt. Three further reserve divisions under OHL control were located around Caudry and Le Cateau, with another two divisions further east around Le Nouvion and two more around Guise.

The mounting Allied pressure was also beginning to fray the German command and control system, with Ludendorff increasingly in conflict with his key staff and army commanders. In August he imposed OHL direction to override Rupprecht's attempts to refine tactical doctrine for defence of the German forward positions. On 6 September, he gave an erratic brief to his *Heeresgruppen* Chiefs of Staff, blaming the troops for the battlefield reverses. He outlined unrealistic plans to construct a new defence line to the rear – the Hermann Stellung – in weeks, when the comparable task of constructing the Hindenburg Line in 1916–17 had taken 65,000 men four months to complete. On 9 September, Oberstleutnant Wetzell, Chief of the OHL Operations Section, resigned after being repeatedly ignored by Ludendorff who increasingly interfered with tactical operations. More spectacularly, General von der Marwitz was relieved of command of 2. Armee on 22 September, after his perceived failure during the battle of Épehy, and replaced by General von Carlowitz. On 23 and 24 September, Wetzell's replacement, Haye, published OHL's latest estimate of the situation which forecast widespread Allied attacks along the whole line, including the Cambrai–St Quentin axis, but suggested that Lorraine remained as the primary threat. None of this augured well for the coming battle.

The St Quentin Canal cutting seen from Riqueval Bridge looking south. This sector was defended by GR 4 of 2. Infanterie-Division. The footbridges were left in place to allow the passage of troops to the forward positions west of the canal. (IWM, Q9510)

THE CAMPAIGN

'AN ABUNDANCE OF COURAGE BUT TOO LITTLE TECHNIQUE', 26 SEPTEMBER

The campaign opened in the early hours as the American First and the French 4e Armies launched their assault on the Meuse, while at St Quentin, Rawlinson's troops began their preparatory bombardment. The French and American infantry assault commenced along a 70km front at 0525hrs, and by the end of the day penetrations up to 7km had been punched through the defences of Heeresgruppe Gallwitz and Heeresgruppe Kronprinz. These were deepest either side of the Argonne forest, however, where the difficult terrain and intricate defences slowed progress. As the key heights at Montfaucon eluded capture, an American Staff Officer, Colonel George C. Marshall, observed that his inexperienced troops had, 'an abundance of courage, but too little technique'.

The battle of the St Quentin Canal

Given the complexity of the defences which faced them, Rawlinson and Monash decided to revert to a preliminary artillery bombardment rather than rely on the surprise bombardments launched at zero hour, which had become the norm in Fourth Army since the battle of Hamel in July. To that end at 2230hrs, 1,044 field and 593 heavy guns crashed the first salvoes intended to disrupt the Hindenburg Line defences, suppress the German artillery and lower morale of the defending troops. The initial phase of the bombardment

BELOW LEFT
American tank units equipped with French FT-17 tanks move forwards in the Argonne. (IWM, Q58691)

BELOW RIGHT
German troops manning a trench while wearing respirators. The Gasschutzmaske Type IV 17 'Gummimaske' and Gasschutzmaske 17 'Ledermaske' both had replaceable filters. Each filter required changing every 20–30 minutes. Note the unprotected dog in the trench. (IWM, Q45349)

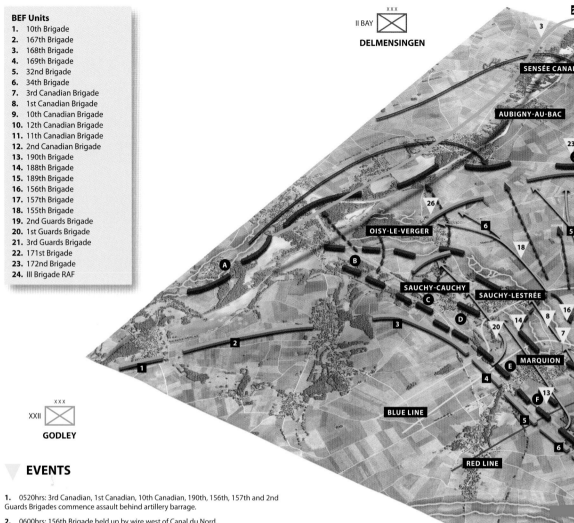

BEF Units
1. 10th Brigade
2. 167th Brigade
3. 168th Brigade
4. 169th Brigade
5. 32nd Brigade
6. 34th Brigade
7. 3rd Canadian Brigade
8. 1st Canadian Brigade
9. 10th Canadian Brigade
10. 12th Canadian Brigade
11. 11th Canadian Brigade
12. 2nd Canadian Brigade
13. 190th Brigade
14. 188th Brigade
15. 189th Brigade
16. 156th Brigade
17. 157th Brigade
18. 155th Brigade
19. 2nd Guards Brigade
20. 1st Guards Brigade
21. 3rd Guards Brigade
22. 171st Brigade
23. 172nd Brigade
24. III Brigade RAF

II BAY
XXX
DELMENSINGEN

SENSÉE CANAL

AUBIGNY-AU-BAC

OISY-LE-VERGER

SAUCHY-CAUCHY

SAUCHY-LESTRÉE

MARQUION

XXII
XXX
GODLEY

BLUE LINE

RED LINE

▼ EVENTS

1. 0520hrs: 3rd Canadian, 1st Canadian, 10th Canadian, 190th, 156th, 157th and 2nd Guards Brigades commence assault behind artillery barrage.

2. 0600hrs: 156th Brigade held up by wire west of Canal du Nord.

3. 0630hrs: III Brigade RAF begins rolling interdiction mission of River Sensée crossing points and Bantigny Valley.

4. 0700–0730hrs: Canadian and 2nd Guards Brigades secure 'Red Line'.

5. 0710hrs: 1st Guards Brigade commences assault on 'Green Line'.

6. 0820hrs: 3rd Canadian, 1st Canadian, 12th Canadian and 11th Canadian Brigades commence assault on 'Green Line'. 188th Brigade passes through 190th Brigade but is held by KSK 30 reserve battalion in 'Sugar Factory'.

7. 0915–1020hrs: Canadian brigades secure 'Green Line' between Bourlon Wood and Marquion.

8. 1020hrs: 12th Canadian, 1st Canadian, 2nd Canadian and 3rd Canadian Brigades commence assault on 'Blue Line'.

9. 1045hrs: GRR 1 launches counter-attack towards Raillencourt. Attack halted along Cambrai–Sauchy railway line under fire from 1st and 12th Canadian Brigades.

10. 1100hrs: IR 82 and IR 167 deploy between Sancourt and Épinoy. IR 83 deploys south-east of Haynecourt. Reserve-Infanterie-Regiment 225 deploys to Graincourt.

11. 1200hrs: 3rd Marine Division deploys to Noyelles.

12. 1215hrs: 3rd Guards Brigade commences assault on 'Blue Line' east of Flesquières.

13. 1220hrs: 32nd and 34th Brigades cross Canal du Nord.

14. 1300hrs: Canadians secure the 'Blue Line'. Marine-Infanterie-Regiments 1, 2 and 3 launch counter-attack towards Flesquières and Anneux.

15. 1345hrs: GRR 2 and RIR 64 launch counter-attack towards Bourlon. Attack held up on Cambrai–Sauchy railway line under fire from 1st and 12th Canadian Brigades. GRR 1 withdrawn to Sailly.

16. 1400hrs: I and II IR 23 launch counter-attack south of Sauchy-Lestrées.

17. 1415–1430hrs: 188th and 189th Brigades finally capture 'Sugar Factory' and advance towards Graincourt and Anneux. 156th and 157th Brigades clear last German resistance west of Graincourt.

18. 1450hrs: 2nd Canadian, 32nd and 34th Brigades commence advance from 'Blue Line'.

19. 1500hrs: 3rd Guards Brigade pushed back from Premy Chapel Ridge.

20. 1550hrs: 169th Brigade crosses the Canal du Nord and begins clearance of eastern bank towards the north.

21. 1600hrs: 171st and 172nd Brigades pass through Graincourt and Anneux and commence assault on 'Blue Line'. MIR 1 holds 171st Brigade east of Anneux. 172nd Brigade advances approximately 1km east of Graincourt before being halted by MIR 2. 172nd Brigade and 3rd Guards Brigade link up.

22. 1650hrs: IR 213 deploys in Proville.

23. 1800hrs: IR 141 deploys east of Épinoy.

24. 1900hrs: 11th Canadian Brigade completes envelopment of Bourlon Wood and secures western edge of Fontaine-Notre-Dame.

25. 1930hrs: 2nd Canadian and 32nd Brigades halt advance in front of German positions held by IRs 141, 82 and 167 between Épinoy and Sancourt.

26. 1945hrs: 34th Brigade secures Oisy-le-Verger. Infanterie-Regiments 107 and 103 withdraw to the river Sensée. Infanterie-Regiment 106 secures Aubigny-au-Bac and bridge.

27. 2000hrs: IR 209 deploys south-east of Fontaine-Notre-Dame.

28. 2230hrs: IR 83 redeploys from Haynecourt to Blécourt.

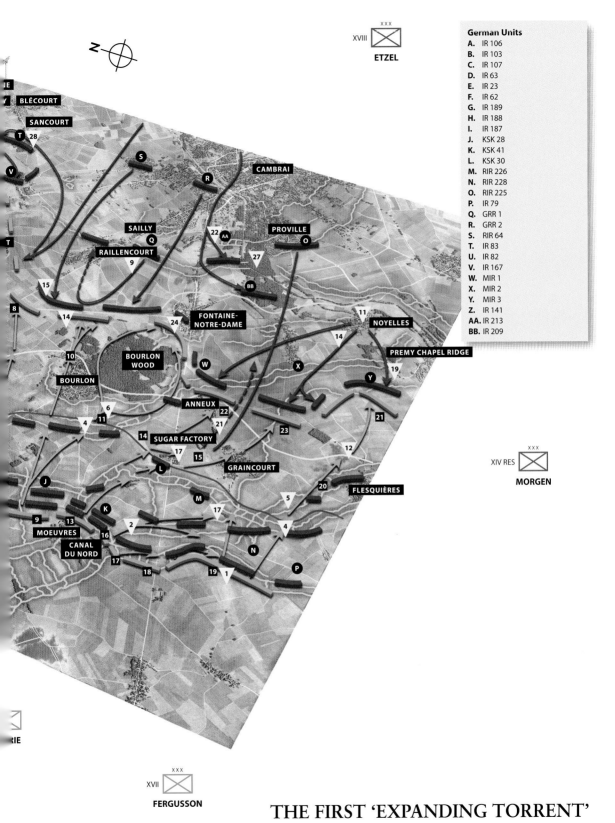

German Units

A. IR 106
B. IR 103
C. IR 107
D. IR 63
E. IR 23
F. IR 62
G. IR 189
H. IR 188
I. IR 187
J. KSK 28
K. KSK 41
L. KSK 30
M. RIR 226
N. RIR 228
O. RIR 225
P. IR 79
Q. GRR 1
R. GRR 2
S. RIR 64
T. IR 83
U. IR 82
V. IR 167
W. MIR 1
X. MIR 2
Y. MIR 3
Z. IR 141
AA. IR 213
BB. IR 209

XVIII — ETZEL

XIV RES — MORGEN

XVII — FERGUSSON

BLÉCOURT
SANCOURT
CAMBRAI
SAILLY
RAILLENCOURT
PROVILLE
FONTAINE-NOTRE-DAME
BOURLON WOOD
BOURLON
ANNEUX
NOYELLES
PREMY CHAPEL RIDGE
SUGAR FACTORY
GRAINCOURT
FLESQUIÈRES
MOEUVRES
CANAL DU NORD

THE FIRST 'EXPANDING TORRENT'
The Canadian and XVII Corps' assault over the Canal du Nord, 27 September 1918

included the first British use of artillery shells filled with mustard gas. The destructive effect was limited, although Reserve Feldartillerie Regiment 55 lost a battery west of Joncourt, with 21 gas casualties. The neutralizing effect, however, was profound as the front-line troops, including those of 2. Infanterie-Division at Bellenglise, were forced to wear their respirators for extended periods or retreat underground where they were cut off from fresh food and water supplies from the rear. The barrage was programmed to continue until zero hour on 29 September, cutting wire in front of the canal, targeting the larger concrete positions, breaching the canal walls and finally destroying the telephone exchanges to break communications.

'ON THIS DAY WE BURIED ALL OUR HOPES OF VICTORY', 27 SEPTEMBER

The second day of the offensive saw the British First and Third Armies launch the second of the attacks at Cambrai, while the previous day's operations continued. The Argonne attack recommenced at 0515hrs with the French push towards Somme-Py. However, the German defence was beginning to firm up, with machine-gun and trench mortar fire presenting stiff resistance to the assaulting infantry. Only a 2–3km advance was made in the east, with none at all in the west. In the American sector, V (US) Corps was able to capture Montfaucon but progress was beginning to slow. The rapid switch from St Mihiel was partly to blame, as Pershing was forced to deploy less well-trained formations, whose inexperienced administrative units were placed under severe pressure to sustain the large force in a remote region with limited transport infrastructure. Furthermore, the divisions deployed on the Meuse suffered from inexperienced leadership from their officers and NCOs, with Gallwitz' men noting that small groups could delay much larger attacking forces.

'Break in' at Cambrai – the battle of the Canal du Nord

At Cambrai, although Third Army's artillery commenced a wire-cutting programme on 18 September, while First Army's guns engaged in deception shoots on XXII Corps' front, no preliminary bombardment on the scale fired by Rawlinson was fired by Horne or Byng. However, fears that the assault troops would be hit by German artillery in their exposed assembly positions proved unfounded. As the assault infantry formed up, the overnight rain cleared. In the distance, the night bomber squadrons of III and IX Brigades RAF attacked those German headquarters that had been identified and Busigny railway junction. At 0520hrs the opening salvoes of the barrage erupted and tore into the German defences. 1st Canadian and 4th Canadian Divisions quickly crossed the dry section of the canal at Inchy-en-Artois and punched through the forward companies of 187 Infanterie-Division to secure the Canal du Nord Line by 0730hrs. Although the German artillery did reply, Horne's deception plan worked, as much fell on the Arras–Cambrai road west of Marquion rather than the Canadians to the

The 16th Canadian Infantry Battalion moving forwards near Inchy-en-Artois. (IWM, CO3289)

south. In XVII Corps, 52nd and 63rd Divisions stormed out of Moeuvres into the forward positions of the 7. Kavallerie-Schützen-Division manning trenches that had formed the original Hindenburg Support Line. Progress was slower than in the Canadian sector, particularly in the area around the 'Sugar Factory' on the Bapaume road, which resisted capture until 1440hrs, long after the Canadians had pushed around the northern flank of Bourlon Wood. Meanwhile, the engineers began the task of bridging the canal. In 4th Canadian Division's sector, three bridges were passable one way for horsed transport by 0800hrs, and the bridge between Inchy and Bourlon was open for two-way lorry transport by 0820hrs. 1st Canadian Division's engineers had more trouble from German fire, but had footbridges open by 1000hrs and a bridge for two-way lorry traffic by 1730hrs. The remainder of 1st Canadian Division, together with 11th British Division, poured over these and swung north, into the rear of 12. and 58. Infanterie-Divisions, who desperately moved back to face the new threat from the south. Some assistance for the defenders came in late morning and early afternoon, when the 1. Garde-Reserve and 22. Infanterie-Divisions counter-attacked from their reserve positions. However, unable to coordinate their efforts, they were absorbed into the battle piecemeal rather than delivering the powerful riposte that was needed to halt Currie's men. Consequently, they found themselves replacing the shattered 7. Kavallerie-Schützen-Division and 187. Infanterie-Division – including IR 188, whose history recorded the catastrophic loss of hope – to re-establish a new left flank for XVIII Armeekorps and cover the north-western approaches to Cambrai. To the south of Bourlon Wood, the final stage of XVII Corps' attack stalled when 57th Division's light signals meant to call the infantry forwards were confused with similar signals fired by the Germans as they launched their own counter-attack towards Anneux. Not until 1800hrs did the 57th move forwards to finish the day 1km east of Graincourt, some 3km behind the foremost Canadian positions to the north.

Canadian engineers bridging the Canal du Nord at Moeuvres. (IWM, Q9638)

Although Byng always intended his army's attack to echelon back towards the right, his plan included a three-hour delay between the assaults of VI and IV Corps in order that the former could advance far enough to re-orientate their subsequent combined attack towards the east rather than north-east. Despite Haldane's protests that the right flank of his corps would be exposed to fire from the high ground in IV Corps' sector as they moved forwards, Harper refused to advance the timing of his attack and Byng decided not to make him do so. This lack of cohesion had significant consequences.

VI Corps commenced their assault in conjunction with XVII Corps at 0520hrs. On the left, the Guards Division cleared the remnants of the Hindenburg Main Line and fought their way across the canal, but thereafter, resistance from 49. Reserve-Division along the junction with XVII Corps and from strongpoints around Flesquières delayed the remainder of the advance. Flesquières, along with the Hindenburg Support Line to the east, was cleared by 3rd Division, and by mid-morning, the 2nd and 62nd Divisions in the corps' second echelon had pushed through to assault the St Quentin Canal at Marcoing. IV Corps launched its assault at 0752hrs with 42nd

CLOSE SUPPORT: FIELD ARTILLERY AT INCHY, 27 SEPTEMBER 1918 (PP. 40–41)

Although the British Army's pre-war artillery doctrine envisaged its field guns deploying amongst the forward infantry positions, their vulnerability to indirect fire from German howitzers soon forced them to seek better protection further to the rear. However, the concept of field guns in the foremost lines did not disappear completely, with the Canadian artillery reiterating the lesson after the battle of Amiens in August. Consequently, when 1st Canadian Infantry Brigade was planning its assault on the Canal du Nord at Inchy, Brig. Griesbach raised concerns over the risk to 1st Canadian Division's overall plan should isolated German machine-gun positions survive bombardment and prevent his troops from seizing crossings over the canal at the opening of the attack. As a result, on 23 September, 1st Canadian Field Artillery Brigade was requested to consider detaching a section (two guns) of 18-pdr field guns to support the 4th Canadian Infantry Battalion by engaging at point-blank range any Germans who survived the barrage. The next day Maj. Drew, commander of 1st Battery, and Lt. Phinney were briefed on the task by Brig. Griesbach and on 26 September the two men carried out a daylight reconnaissance to assess the feasibility of the request and select firing positions. In the process, they came under heavy machine-gun fire from the forward positions of 8. Kompanie, Infanterie-Regiment 188, dug in around the western abutment of the demolished bridge east of Inchy. This highlighted the threat to the attack and the necessity of the close support task. The plan was agreed and confirmed by orders that evening.

Lieutenant Phinney, together with the leaders of each gun team, Sgt. Cousins and Cpl. Warren, prepared the teams for the approach march by muffling the hooves and harnesses of the horses and the wheels of their guns (1). They moved forwards in the early hours of 27 September. Despite their precautions, they were detected and came under heavy German machine-gun and artillery fire as they occupied positions in front of the Canadian infantry outpost line, only 150m from the German positions. However, under Phinney's cool leadership they were ready at 0540hrs, when the field artillery and heavy artillery brigades commenced the barrage to open the attack. Initially this fell between the German and the Canadians lines, but by 0546hrs it had lifted onto the eastern bank of the canal and exposed the surviving Germans in the outposts on the western bank. Phinney's men immediately engaged as the troops of D Company, 4th Canadian Infantry Battalion, advanced (2). Green 'SOS' rockets were fired by the Germans (3) and some protective artillery fire began to fall around Inchy but to little avail. By 0552hrs, D Company had secured the canal line with their morale lifted by the sight of Phinney's section pounding 50 rounds into 8. Kompanie's positions in that short space of time. Their mission complete, Phinney's guns re-joined their battery at 0620hrs as it advanced past them to cross the canal and continue the attack.

and 5th Divisions, but 113. Infanterie-Division, alerted by the earlier attacks to the north, put up fierce resistance. Nine of the 12 tanks supporting the attack were quickly knocked out and heavy machine-gun fire raked the infantry. Subsequent German counter-attacks held Highland Ridge, from where, as predicted by Haldane, they turned their attention onto VI Corps to the north. Although the forward troops of 2nd and 62nd Divisions got as far as Premy Chapel, resistance from the flank thinned their numbers before a counter-attack by 3. Marine-Division threw them back. By nightfall Third Army had cleared the Main and Support Hindenburg Lines north of Ribécourt and overlooked the intermediate defences between Marcoing and Bourlon. To the south, however, the Schelde Canal had not been crossed and the Hindenburg Line on its west bank remained in German possession.

Fixing 24lb Cooper bombs to a Sopwith Camel. Although the Germans developed specialized ground attack aircraft, the British response for close air support was to arm single-seat fighters with these weapons. Each was filled with 4lb of Amatol HE. (IWM, CO2856)

In the air, contact aircraft from the corps wings were above the battle by 0550hrs, reporting on German batteries in action and controlling the British artillery response. Although III Brigade limited its ground attack effort to one fighter squadron during the day, I Brigade launched five fighter squadrons under a unified command at the Sensée crossings up to Wasnes-au-Bac. Above them two bomber squadrons also attacked the same town, while the bomber squadrons of IX Brigade RAF attacked the German airfields at Bertry and Bévillers, which resulted in heavy fighting between the escorts and the defending Jastas.

Stalemate on the outpost line – the battle of the St Quentin Canal

In contrast to the shattering blow delivered by the British and Canadians crossing the Canal du Nord, Fourth Army struggled to resolve the difficulties caused by III Corps' failure to capture the Advanced Hindenburg Line north of Hargicourt during the battle of Épehy. Rawlinson refused Monash's request to commence the main attack from the line currently held, and slipping the date was impossible. It was therefore decided that three battalions of the American 106th Regiment would complete this task as a preliminary operation to the main assault. At 0530hrs, they advanced on a 4km front behind a creeping barrage fired by nine brigades of artillery and supported by 12 tanks. Critically, however, only 18 officers were available to lead the troops of 12 companies due to the remainder being absent for centralized training with the rest of the American Army. Despite early success in breaking into the German positions, command and control began to break apart as the casualties mounted. Determined and skilful counter-attacks by the troops of 54. and 121. Infanterie-Divisions in Conta's IV Reservekorps, drove the Americans back, and by mid-morning the Germans re-possessed the key posts of 'The Knoll', 'Gillemont Farm' and 'Quennemont Farm'. American casualties amounted to 1,540, including 17 of the 18 officers. In IX Corps, 46th Division executed a minor operation to improve their line of departure for the coming attack west of Bellenglise, capturing over 100 men from 2. Infanterie-Division.

In the French sector, Debeney began to concentrate his forces in preparation for their assault north of St Quentin. At 1800hrs 15e Corps headquarters handed over command of 60e Division to 8e Corps and

The battle of the Canal du Nord

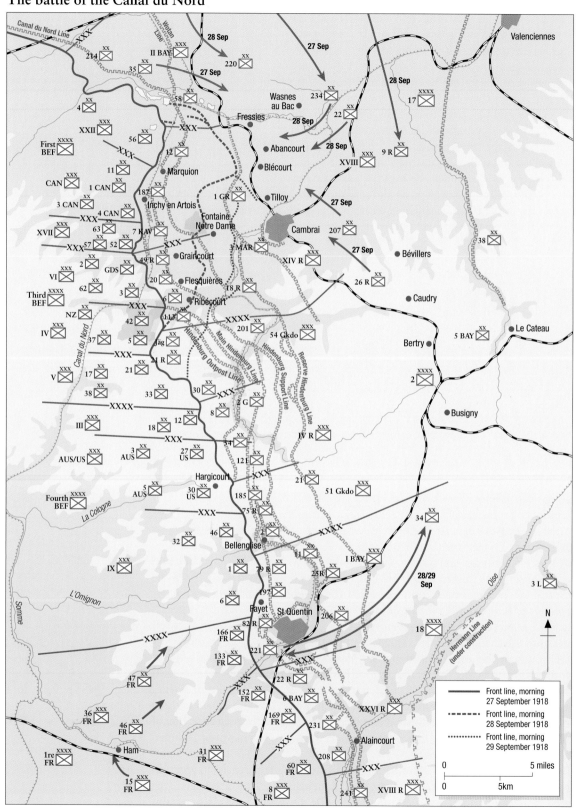

withdrew to take over command of 46e, 47e and 126e Divisions in the rear. 15e Corps would then move north to deploy on the boundary of the British and French armies around Fayet.

Command decisions

In response to the day's events, the Germans began to redeploy their units. Heeresgruppe Rupprecht was in the process of withdrawing 207. Infanterie-Division from 6. Armee to reinforce 17. Armee. This move began the day before, but now assumed a far greater urgency despite being disrupted by a single British long-range heavy artillery shell, which killed or injured 69 troops from Infanterie-Regiment 213 as they passed through Douai. By evening, however, the division was beginning to deploy west of Cambrai with XVIII Armeekorps. In addition, 9. Reserve-Division was also ordered to redeploy from 6. Armee south of Lille to 17. Armee. Within 17. Armee itself, 234. Infanterie-Division at Douai and 35. Infanterie-Division at Arras were detached from I and II Bayerische Armeekorps respectively and sent to XVIII Armeekorps, to back up 22. and 12. Infanterie-Divisions between Abancourt and Fressies. These reinforcements were augmented by the 26. Reserve-Division, released from its holding position around Le Cateau by OHL. No reinforcement was directed to 2. Armee, where the troops of IV. Reservekorps were celebrating their successful battle with food liberated from the Americans' packs and reporting their impressions of the new enemy. Meanwhile, to the south the German 7. Armee began to withdraw from Mangin's 10e Armée on the Chemin des Dames and take up positions behind the Aisne-Oise Canal between Soissons and Laon.

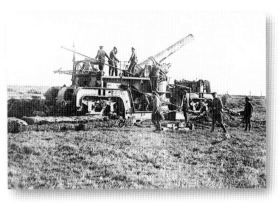

BL 12in. Mk. V Railway Howitzer, 'Peeping Tom', ready to fire in support of First Army on 27 September 1918. Built by the Elswick Ordnance Company on Tyneside from May 1917, each gun weighed 60 tons and could fire a 750lb shell 15,000 yards. First Army had ten of these weapons for the battle. (IWM, Q64698)

'THE WHOLE OPERATION WENT LIKE CLOCKWORK', 28 SEPTEMBER

The following day, the GAF entered the fray in Flanders, while the Meuse-Argonne battle struggled forwards against increasingly resolute defence, and the Germans desperately attempted to check the BEF on the Hindenburg Line.

At 0530hrs the British Second and Belgian Armies of the GAF attacked on a 30km front between Dixmude and Ploegsteert. Despite the shattered nature of the terrain, they quickly seized their objectives, and by the end of the day the Passchendaele Ridge, which had taken four months' hard fighting to capture the previous year, was in their hands. The BEF's 9th Division diary recorded with satisfaction that the attack '...went like clockwork'. The French and Americans were not so fortunate in the Meuse-Argonne. During the morning, 4e Armée units penetrated Somme-Py only to be ejected by an aggressive counter-attack by two German divisions. Although they retook the town later in the day, gains were limited. In the American sector, a final effort saw III (US) Corps

American transport in a traffic jam. The decision to prioritize infantry and machine-gunners to be transported to France in the spring and summer of 1918, meant that not all divisions in the AEF had a fully trained logistic support component by 26 September. (IWM, Q70736)

close up to the Kreimhild Line, but I (US) Corps was entangled in the wild terrain of the Argonne Forest as the American First Army's administrative services finally broke down. The operational contribution of the Meuse-Argonne attack to the Allied offensive, however, was way above its tactical achievement, as six of the German reserve divisions released from Alsace-Lorraine had been sucked into this battle.

Reinforcements arrive – the battle of the Canal du Nord

Overnight both British and German commanders desperately attempted to reorganize their forces and continue the battle. Byng's Third Army gave orders to continue the mission of the previous day and seize the crossings over the Schelde Canal. His corps would attack in sequence once more, but this time, IV Corps on the right would step off first. At 0230hrs the 5th and 42nd Divisions resumed their assault and succeeded in driving the defenders off Highland Ridge, although 5th Division faced more serious opposition in the vicinity of Villers Plouich. At 0515hrs, VI Corps recommenced its advance over the open terrain north of Marcoing, extending its attack at 0630hrs to the whole corps frontage. The Cantaing Line was quickly overcome, but only at Marcoing could a foothold be gained on the far bank of the canal. On the left, 2nd Division could only cover the remaining bridges and locks but in so doing prevented the Germans from demolishing them. Fergusson's XVII Corps attacked at 0615hrs with 57th Division in the lead, supported by 63rd Division. By 0830hrs the Cantaing Line had been secured, and at 1100hrs, the attempt to cross the canal began. Again, however, determined German resistance slowed progress and only small parties were able to establish themselves on the far bank.

North of the Cambrai–Bapaume road, Horne also ordered the Canadians to push forwards and endeavour to cross the Schelde Canal, although Currie still had to reorganize his forces as they fanned out beyond the narrow bridgehead seized the previous day. 3rd Canadian Division was to be brought into the line on the right flank, while the Canadian Independent Force – comprising motorized machine-gun units – was prepared to exploit the advance beyond the canal if the opportunity arose. As the right of the corps was behind the left, 3rd and 4th Canadian Divisions advanced at 0600hrs under an artillery bombardment, and although Fontaine-Notre-Dame was captured, the resistance of 1 Garde-Reserve-Division and 207. Infanterie-Division resolutely held the western approaches to Cambrai. Attack and counter-attack from 1000hrs onwards saw the Canadians establish footholds in the forward trenches of the Marcoing Line, but heavy casualties meant that they could not develop them further. On the left, 1st Canadian Division attacked alone at 0900hrs, but following difficulties in coordinating the artillery barrage with the infantry, it made little progress. Further north, however, the withdrawal of II Bayerische Armeekorps' left flank behind the Sensée, allowed patrols from 11th and 56th Divisions to cover the canal and occupy Palluel. Throughout the day, German reinforcements began to arrive on the battlefield, with the leading regiments of 26. Reserve-Division taking up positions around Blécourt and Tilloy from mid-morning onwards,

Overnight, IX Brigade RAF attacked Busigny Junction once more, dropping 6 tons of bombs on the target. I Brigade RAF reduced its ground attack efforts from the previous day by re-tasking two of the five squadrons to conduct offensive patrols against German observation balloons and aircraft. The remainder kept a close watch on German reserves moving into the battlezone, with a patrol from 209 Squadron disrupting a large column heading towards Cambrai from Le Cateau in the evening.

'In a state of despair' – the battle of the St Quentin Canal

Meanwhile, in Fourth Army, as the reports of the previous day's fighting were analysed, it had become apparent that the American preliminary attack had misfired and that the Advanced Hindenburg Line would not be secured as the line of departure for the main assault. Conferences were held to determine whether the planned barrage would be adjusted to the new situation, when news was received from the supporting aircraft that American survivors were pinned down around the forward German positions. The prospect of shelling his own men appalled O'Ryan, and consequently Monash asked Rawlinson to delay the main assault for 24 hours. This proved impossible without disrupting the wider synchronization of the General Offensive now in full swing. Therefore, as the lesser of two evils, Monash and O'Ryan agreed to attack as planned, with the supporting barrage now some 1,000m ahead of the assaulting infantry and beyond the German front-line positions. In an attempt to alleviate some of the developing threat to the Americans, Rawlinson allocated additional tanks to support them, but Monash told Haig, who was visiting his Corps HQ, that he was in 'a state of despair'.

On the German side of the lines, in an effort to evade the ongoing British artillery barrage, Carlowitz' gunners began to shift their battery positions to new and undetected sites. Furthermore, at 0600hrs, 2. Infanterie-Division counter-attacked behind a heavy barrage in an attempt to retake the positions lost the previous day. The outposts of the 46th Division were cut off from their supporting troops and engaged in hard fighting throughout the morning. Although the Germans were unable to eject the British by force, by the time the attack petered out they had made the position untenable. Consequently, the 46th Division withdrew overnight to its original trenches.

Command decisions

The stiffening German defence in front of First Army had blocked the opportunity for the Canadian Independent Force to seize crossings over the Schelde Canal around Escaudoeuvres and open a way for the cavalry. Likewise, Third Army had been unable to open crossings over the Schelde Canal around Marcoing. With First Army having been checked, Haig redeployed Kavanagh's Cavalry Corps to the rear of Fourth Army to support Rawlinson instead, although the cavalry remained under GHQ's control.

In Heeresgruppe Rupprecht, the new attack in Flanders, in addition to the attack already underway at Cambrai, now threatened the potential encirclement of 6. Armee and 17. Armee. As a result, while two reserve divisions were immediately sucked into the battle on the Passchendaele Ridge, another six were retained east of Ypres to block any subsequent breakthrough, where they were joined by 1 Bayerische-Reserve-Division sent north from Lens. Only 220. Infanterie-Division was sent south to the battle at Cambrai. Meanwhile, Boehn remained apprehensive of the threat to his Army Group's right flank as 17. Armee was driven back south of Cambrai. As a result, he persuaded OHL to release 38. Infanterie-Division and 5. Bayerische-Division from Caudry and Le Cateau, from where they

Bombing raid on Caudry sidings, 24 September 1918. The attacks against the German rail network were an essential component of the Allied campaign, totally undermining Ludendorff's ability to redeploy his reserves from Alsace-Lorraine. (IWM, HU 131793)

prepared to reinforce XIV Reservekorps. This move sucked the final reserves on the flanks between 17. and 2. Armeen into the battle around Cambrai. Meanwhile, Larisch gave orders for 54. Generalkommando to evacuate Gouzeaucourt and conform to XIV Reservekorps to the north.

On a wider scale Ludendorff's ability to reposition his forces was beginning to unravel at an accelerating rate. OHL's scheme to transfer 12 reserve divisions from Alsace-Lorraine to the west was now in disarray, as the overstretched railways began to break down under the extreme demands placed upon them. Only seven of the reserve divisions had been able to cross the Meuse, of which six had been absorbed into the Meuse-Argonne battle and the last had gone to Flanders. The remaining five divisions, together with the nine divisions that were being retained east of the Meuse, represented 20 per cent of Ludendorff's Western Front reserves, and were now isolated in Alsace-Lorraine, where they would not be available for the developing battle. It was a loss of strength that Ludendorff could ill afford.

If this situation was bad, then in the afternoon it got much worse, with news that the Bulgarians were seeking a separate peace following the Allied offensive in the Balkans. Some reports suggest that Ludendorff had a temporary physical breakdown when told. By the evening, however, he had recovered enough to discuss the situation with Hindenburg. Both were in agreement that an armistice with the Allies must be sought immediately, and an audience with the Kaiser was arranged for 1000hrs the next day at Spa to discuss the crisis.

'AS FAR AS THE EYE COULD SEE, OUR TROOPS WERE PUSHING FORWARD', 29 SEPTEMBER

Even as the German commanders prepared to brief their Sovereign, the situation on the battlefield deteriorated still further. Throughout the early hours of the morning, the British First and Third Armies continued the attack at Cambrai, while further south, Rawlinson's Fourth Army assembled for the climactic assault. On the Meuse-Argonne front, the American First Army began the process of rehabilitating its disorganized units. Meanwhile, the French 4e Armée moved forwards once more, but with diminishing strength in difficult country, with only limited gains made north-east of Somme-Py. At Ypres the GAF continued to fight its way across the Passchendaele Ridge. The British Second Army advanced between Messines and Broodseinde, and by the end of the day had forces on the river Lys south of Comines to further threaten the north-western approaches to Lille.

'The brave Grenadiers stand like a wall' – the battle of the Canal du Nord

As the German troops pulled back, the Third Army extended its attack to include V Corps for the first time, assaulting in conjunction with IV Corps to the north at 0330hrs. However, the German withdrawal had not been

The battles of the Canal du Nord and St Quentin Canal

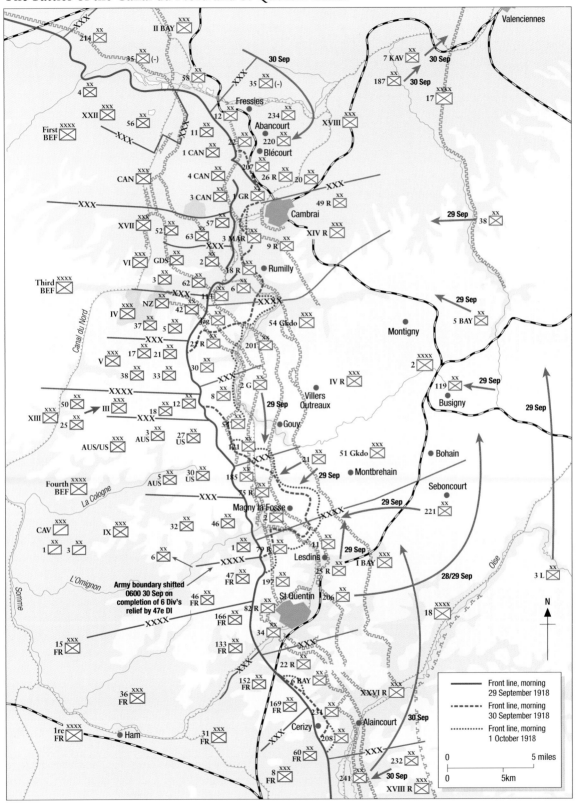

Valenciennes

Fressies
Abancourt
Blécourt
Cambrai
Rumilly
Montigny
Busigny
Villers Outreaux
Gouy
Bohain
Montbrehain
Magny la Fosse
Seboncourt
Lesdins
St Quentin
Cerizy
Alaincourt
Ham

Canal du Nord
La Cologne
L'Omignon
Somme
Oise

Army boundary shifted 0600 30 Sep on completion of 6 Div's relief by 47e DI

N

	Front line, morning 29 September 1918
	Front line, morning 30 September 1918
	Front line, morning 1 October 1918

0   5 miles
0   5km

49

Canadian Motor Machine
Gun unit from the Canadian
Independent Force on
the Arras–Cambrai road.
(IWM, CO3363)

followed up, and both 33rd and 21st Divisions found Villers-Guislain and Gonnelieu now strongly held by Larisch's 54. Generalkommando. Harper's IV Corps had better luck, as the New Zealand Division was able to capture La Vaquerie and clear the Hindenburg Support Line to the northeast. In VI Corps, 2nd and 62nd Divisions were able to push 3. Marine-Division and 6. Infanterie-Division back across the Schelde Canal and seize the Marcoing Line defences south of Rumilly, but a counter-attack by 9. Reserve-Division as it came into line prevented the British from pushing further east. XVII Corps was able to clear the Marcoing Line west of the Schelde Canal and established pontoon bridges to cross the canal, but stiffening resistance by 3. Marine-Division held it on the south-western outskirts of Cambrai.

General Horne again ordered First Army to cross the Schelde Canal north-east of Cambrai and open the way for the Canadian Independent Force. Currie's Canadians advanced at 0800hrs for a day of bitter fighting against Etzell's XVIII Armeekorps. On the right, 3rd Canadian Division captured St Olle and pushed 1. Garde-Reserve-Division back onto the north-western outskirts of Cambrai, where Garde-Reserve-Regiment 1 formed its human wall. To the north, 4th Canadian Division embarked on a titanic struggle against the combined efforts of 26. Reserve, 207. and 22. Infanterie-Divisions, but despite breaking into Blécourt and Sancourt, German counter-attacks were able to retake both villages. Difficulties in coordinating the artillery with the infantry of 1st Canadian Division prevented any success, and neither they nor 11th Division to their left could make any progress.

Annihilation at Bellenglise – the battle of the St Quentin Canal

While the earlier attacks ground their way forwards, the British Fourth Army prepared to join the fray at St Quentin. Overnight, Rawlinson's troops filed into their assault positions. The rain of the previous days had cleared up, but a thick autumn mist began to form in the early hours of the morning. This did not hinder the night bomber squadrons of IX Brigade RAF as they attacked the fortified villages of Villers Outreaux and Fresnoy-le-Grand, and the rail junctions at Bohain and Busigny.

On the left of Fourth Army, 27th (US) Division prepared to move off at 0450hrs, one hour ahead of the main attack, in a final attempt to seize the Advanced Hindenburg Line. Maj. Gen. O'Ryan's plan envisaged 107th Regiment attacking on the left, with 108th Regiment on the right. 105th Regiment would provide flank protection on the left, while 106th Regiment would mop up any remaining positions. As the New Yorkers made their final preparations, six tanks of the British 4th Tank Battalion set out slightly early and, without any infantry support, attacked the forward positions of 54. and 121. Infanterie-Divisions. They returned having done little more than alert the defenders and lost one of their number that strayed into an old British minefield in the process. The American attack, supported by 34 tanks of 301st (US) Tank Battalion, was too far from its protective artillery barrage and met a hail of artillery and machine-gun fire from the Germans. Although the initial assault appeared to make progress and broke into the forward positions, heavy losses, including 12 tanks destroyed by anti-tank guns and two destroyed in the same minefield as the British tank, drained momentum. The German counter-attack companies then struck back and by 0900hrs had re-established the defensive line. As 3rd Australian Division moved forwards around Ronssoy, expecting to pass through the Americans 3km further ahead, they were stopped by German shells bursting around them and heard the familiar rattle of machine-gun fire in the near distance.

A Mk. V tank disabled in a minefield in front of 'Duncan Post'. The minefield was made up of British 'plum pudding' trench mortar bombs, dug into the ground with their contact fuses pointing up. Each weapon had 12.5lb (5.6kg) of amatol or ammonal HE filling. (IWM, E(AUS) 4939)

On their left in III Corps, 12th Division held the whole corps front, while 18th Division advanced from the American sector to approach Vendhuille from the south. 54th Brigade moved across 'The Knoll' to its first objective, where it held off counter-attacks from Infanterie-Regiment 84. However, as 55th Brigade commenced the next move north to clear Vendhuille, it was ordered to halt by its commander when heavy machine-gun fire swept across its front, and remained stationary for the next four hours.

30th (US) Division had better luck, as their possession of the Advanced Hindenburg Line allowed them a clear run at the Main Hindenburg Line defences. Although 185. Infanterie- and 75. Reserve-Divisions had extemporised a new outpost line in old communication trenches, the thick fog greatly assisted the Americans. Unlike 27th (US) Division, the men from the Carolinas and Tennessee hugged their protective barrage as they fought their way forward. Although 119th Regiment came under fire from the unsuppressed German positions to their north, they formed a protective flank facing that direction, while 120th Regiment pushed Infanterie-Regiment 65 and Reserve-Infanterie-Regiment 251 back though Bellicourt and drove on towards Nauroy.

On Rawlinson's right, however, IX Corps' attack was a stunning success. 46th Division was chosen to spearhead the operation, commanded by Maj. Gen. Gerald Boyd. Commissioned from the ranks in the Boer War, Boyd had prepared his men thoroughly for the task ahead. In anticipation of the coming assault, he ordered the requisition of 3,000 life jackets and life belts from the cross-Channel steamers, along with collapsible boats to equip his men. Cork mats were to be used to cross sections of canal mired in deep mud. On 27 and 28 September, he conducted a full rehearsal, with his troops swimming the moat at Brie Chateau in full assault order. Individuals who could not swim were taught to use lifelines to pull themselves along.

Mark V tanks moving forwards with the 5th Australian Division at Bellicourt, 29 September 1918. The wooden 'cribs' on their roofs were designed to be dropped into the wide and deep Hindenburg Line trenches to allow the tanks to cross. (IWM, Q9364)

Facing them was GenMaj. von Dommes' 2. Infanterie-Division, which entered the line on 19 September having fought through the August battles in Picardy. On 24 September it was reinforced by Reserve-Infanterie-Regiment 373 from the disbanded 225. Infanterie-Division, which allowed his battalions to resume a four-company structure. Like his counterparts to the north, despite losing possession of the Advanced Hindenburg Line, he

The St Quentin Canal at Bellenglise looking north. (IWM, Q55626)

Infantry Company HQ from 10th Australian Brigade in trenches near Gillemont Farm, 29 September 1918. (IWM, E(AUS) 3478)

had chosen to hold ground west of the canal, placing his forward companies some 500m beyond it. Following the minor operations of the preceding days, Dommes decided to improve the security of the canal line by pulling forward one of his rear battalions from its positions protecting the artillery at Magny-la-Fosse, and redeploying it in the Bellenglise Tunnel. He replaced it with two platoons from one of the forward battalions. Consequently, of his 36 infantry companies, 16 were in the forward trenches, 14 and a half were hunkered down in the tunnels and bunkers around the village and canal as the bombardment crashed over them, and five and a half were protecting the artillery in front of Magny-la-Fosse. His command therefore had the majority of its strength covering the canal, but it was a perilously thin crust and dangerously exposed to the full weight of the British artillery. His local reserves were very limited and the *Eingrief* divisions were too far away to intervene quickly.

As in the Australian Corps sector, a thick fog enveloped the battlefield when, at 0550hrs, nine brigades of heavy artillery and ten brigades of field artillery opened an intense barrage to support the assault. Following closely behind, the troops of 137th Brigade stormed forward between Bellenglise and the Riqueval Bridge and overwhelmed the German positions west of the canal whose ability to fight back was severely restricted by the limited visibility. On the left of the attack, a party of the 6th North Staffordshire Regiment seized the bridge as German Pioneers attempted to demolish it, while further south the leading troops began to cross the canal by swimming, using mud mats and by utilizing footbridges and concrete dams that had been left intact by the Germans. After a short pause to reconsolidate on the east bank, the second-wave companies took over the fight to clear the village where they found that the western entrance of the Bellenglise Tunnel had been blocked by 12in. shellfire in the preceding days. Some resistance came from isolated machine-gun posts and a nearby battery of field guns, but the fog continued to blind their crews and the positions were cleared at close range by bayonet and grenade. By 0820hrs 137th Brigade had secured the bridgehead over the canal. To the south of Bellenglise, 1st Division advanced to cover the right of 46th Division. 1st and 3rd Brigades had little difficulty driving back the right and centre of 79. Reserve-Division and were soon on their objective on the St Quentin–Bellenglise road.

In response to the attack Boehn's commanders began their counter-moves. In IV Reservekorps, Conta ordered 2. Garde-Division to move forwards from Clary, while 51. Generalkommando called forwards 21. Infanterie-Division from Prémont. Further east, 119. Infanterie-Division was brought to increased readiness by OHL. In I Bayerische Armeekorps on the right flank of 18. Armee, Endres observed that the attack front did not extend beyond 79. Reserve-Division's sector but continued to wait until the situation became clearer before committing his reserve units.

In the Australian Corps sector, the troops of 3rd and 5th Australian Divisions were becoming increasingly aware that something had gone wrong. Although ordered not to become embroiled in the American tasks, the disorganized situation that unfolded before them gave them little option but to do so, as 9th, 10th and 11th Australian Brigades began to gather up the American survivors and reorganize the attack. 10th Australian Brigade attempted to make its way forwards and clear Gillemont Farm, but the resistance of Reserve-Infanterie-Regiment 90 was firm and held them off. To their south, 44th Battalion of 11th Brigade and 59th Battalion of 15th Brigade on the left of 5th Australian Division became intermingled in the poor visibility, but seized the opportunity to close in on Quennemont Farm and finally overcome the garrison from Reserve-Infanterie-Regiment 56. Having done so, they pushed east until reaching the spoil mound which ran above the line of the Bellicourt Tunnel, where they were stopped by artillery and machine-gun fire. At this point, a company each from 17th Armoured Car and 6th Tank Battalion arrived at Quennemont Farm and advanced towards Bony, where intense machine-gun and anti-tank gun fire destroyed eight of the 18 vehicles involved before they were hurriedly withdrawn to safety.

8th Australian Brigade on 5th Australian Division's right groped their way forwards through the fog to find that the Main Hindenburg Line on their front had been cleared by 30th (US) Division before they had lost momentum against the German defences. The Australians passed through Bellicourt and pressed on towards Nauroy. Having passed through the foremost American troops, they proceeded to assault the village, only to be stopped in their tracks by the fire of Batteries 8 and 9 of Feldartillerie-Regiment 55 and the remnants of Reserve-Infanterie-Regiment 251. Despite having their supporting tanks destroyed, 29th Battalion worked their way forwards and broke into the trenches of the Hindenburg Support Line, running across the western edge of the village. Turning north, they cleared the gun positions that had caused the trouble, but did not go further into the village. On their right, 32nd Battalion, supported by two tanks, swept south of the village, which was secured by 30th Battalion as they followed up.

In IX Corps, under cover of a protective artillery barrage, engineers from 46th and 32nd Divisions cleared the Riqueval Bridge, adapted a concrete dam to take transport and erected pontoon bridges over the canal. Sensing the disarray in the German defences on the canal, Maj. Gen. Boyd telephoned IX Corps and requested 5th Cavalry Brigade to move forwards from its holding area in preparation to exploit his division's success. Meanwhile, 138th and 139th Brigades moved forwards through the fog in preparation of the breakout from the bridgehead.

The poor visibility limited the effectiveness of the support given by the aircraft of IX and V Brigades RAF, but significant aerial engagements were fought throughout the morning. Around

German infantry with a Skoda 75mm Gebirgskanone 15. These were bought by Germany when trying to equip their infantry with a direct support weapon. They were used as anti-tank guns at the end of the war, but they lacked the muzzle velocity to be truly effective in this role. (IWM, Q54414)

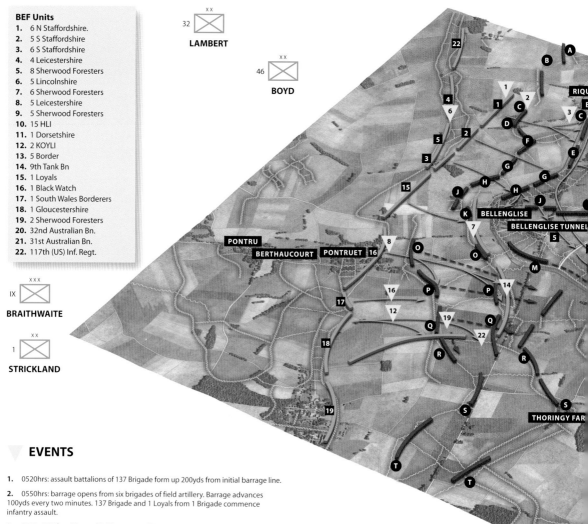

BEF Units
1. 6 N Staffordshire.
2. 5 S Staffordshire
3. 6 S Staffordshire
4. 4 Leicestershire
5. 8 Sherwood Foresters
6. 5 Lincolnshire
7. 6 Sherwood Foresters
8. 5 Leicestershire
9. 5 Sherwood Foresters
10. 15 HLI
11. 1 Dorsetshire
12. 2 KOYLI
13. 5 Border
14. 9th Tank Bn
15. 1 Loyals
16. 1 Black Watch
17. 1 South Wales Borderers
18. 1 Gloucestershire
19. 2 Sherwood Foresters
20. 32nd Australian Bn.
21. 31st Australian Bn.
22. 117th (US) Inf. Regt.

32 LAMBERT

46 BOYD

IX BRAITHWAITE

1 STRICKLAND

▼ EVENTS

1. 0520hrs: assault battalions of 137 Brigade form up 200yds from initial barrage line.

2. 0550hrs: barrage opens from six brigades of field artillery. Barrage advances 100yds every two minutes. 137 Brigade and 1 Loyals from 1 Brigade commence infantry assault.

3. 0615–0625hrs: Riqueval Bridge captured intact. 137 Brigade storms the canal line.

4. 0730hrs: trenches immediately east of the canal cleared.

5. 0820hrs: Bellenglise village and tunnel cleared. 'Brown Line' on ridgeline east of canal secured. 137th Brigade consolidate positions while engineers begin construction of bridges over canal.

6. 0830hrs: 138th and 139th Brigades advance from holding position to pass through 137 Brigade.

7. 0840hrs: 1 Loyals clear trenches south-west of canal and link up with 6 S Staffordshire in Bellenglise.

8. 1000hrs: 1 Black Watch begin to clear German trenches east of Pontruet.

9. 1105hrs: link established with US infantry from 117th Regiment clearing the east bank of the canal from the north.

10. 1120hrs: 4 Leicestershire and 8 Sherwood Foresters commence 138 and 139 Brigades' assault to 'Yellow Line'. Two companies from 9th Tank Battalion join the attack having crossed the canal at Bellicourt. I/10 conduct a fighting withdrawal to the east along trenches on northern bank of the canal.

11. 1130hrs: 4 Leicestershire link up with Australian 32nd Battalion as it advances from the north.

12. 1140hrs: 1 Black Watch and 1 Gloucestershire assault east and south of Pontruet. Heavy artillery and machine-gun fire from RIR 263 and RFAR 63 stall Gloucestershire attack 250yds from German positions.

13. 1220hrs: 5 Lincolnshire and 6 Sherwood Foresters take over assault from 'Yellow Line'. 2 Batterie/RFAR 63 destroys tanks from C Coy, 9th Tank Battalion. Sherwood Foresters re-cross the canal to kill or capture German gun crews.

14. 1300hrs: 1 Black Watch clears trenches west of the Bellenglise–St Quentin road.

15. 1320hrs: 5 Leicestershire and 5 Sherwood Foresters take over assault from 'Blue Dotted Line'. 'Green Line' reached at 1410hrs and line consolidated.

16. 1500hrs: 1 South Wales Borderers advance and secure German trenches west of the Bellenglise–St Quentin road.

17. 1500hrs: 32nd Australian Battalion halts south of Joncourt. Patrols deployed north and east; flank thrown back to link up with 31st Australian Battalion in Etricourt.

18. 1600hrs: IR 80 advances through Joncourt and occupies defensive positions on spurs facing Etricourt and Magny-la-Fosse after receiving heavy fire from 32nd Australian Battalion and 5 Leicestershire.

19. 1730hrs: 1 Gloucestershire seize the German front-line trench with an attack from the left flank.

20. 1800hrs: 14th and 97th Brigades pass through 46th Division's troops and launch 32nd Division's assault on Le Tronquoy–Levergies–Joncourt Ridge.

21. 1800hrs: IR 38, II/10 and III/10 arrive in Levergies. Defensive positions set up on railway to the west and flank extended to south-west in order to link up with Le Tronquoy position.

22. 1830hrs: 1 Gloucestershire secure the ridgeline overlooking Bellenglise from the south.

23. 1830hrs: heavy fire from Levergies and Joncourt halts 5 Border and 2 KOYLI. Lehaucourt Ridge becomes front line at nightfall.

24. 2030hrs: 15 HLI clear Le Tronquoy from an ad hoc German force consisting of command and admin personnel together with survivors withdrawing from earlier fighting to the west. 1 Dorsetshire are repulsed by fire from Levergies and throw back a defensive left flank at nightfall to link with 2 KOYLI to the north.

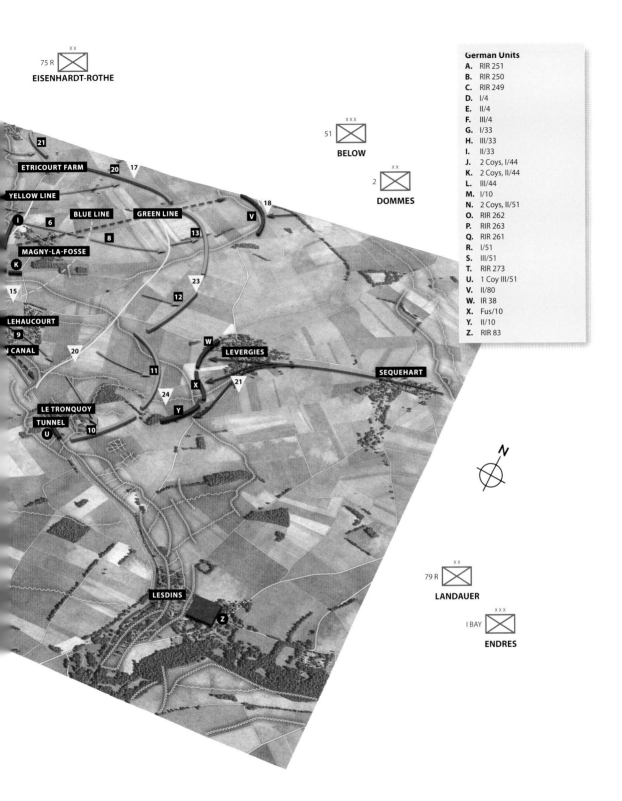

EISENHARDT-ROTHE
75 R

BELOW
51

DOMMES
2

21
ETRICOURT FARM
20 17
YELLOW LINE
I 6 BLUE LINE GREEN LINE
V
8 13
MAGNY-LA-FOSSE
K
18
15
23
12
LEHAUCOURT
9
J CANAL
20
11
W
LEVERGIES
24
X 21
Y
LE TRONQUOY
TUNNEL
U 10

SEQUEHART

LESDINS
Z

LANDAUER
79 R

I BAY
ENDRES

N

German Units

A.	RIR 251
B.	RIR 250
C.	RIR 249
D.	I/4
E.	II/4
F.	III/4
G.	I/33
H.	III/33
I.	II/33
J.	2 Coys, I/44
K.	2 Coys, II/44
L.	III/44
M.	I/10
N.	2 Coys, II/51
O.	RIR 262
P.	RIR 263
Q.	RIR 261
R.	I/51
S.	III/51
T.	RIR 273
U.	1 Coy III/51
V.	II/80
W.	IR 38
X.	Fus/10
Y.	II/10
Z.	RIR 83

BREAKING THE HINDENBURG LINE
IX Corps' assault at Bellenglise, 29 September 1918

Urvillers from the west. The village formed part of the Allied reserve trench lines in 1917, which were re-fortified by the Germans as they fell back to the Hindenburg Line in September 1918. The German trenches ran from left to right across the forward edge of the village. 169e Division took 510 prisoners from 6. Bayerische- and 231. Infanterie-Divisions in capturing the village. (Author)

0900hrs, DH9 bombers of 27 Squadron struck again at the rail junction of Busigny and were attacked by the Fokker DVIIs of Jasta 5. Shortly afterwards, at 0940hrs, the DH9s of 98 Squadron attacked the airbase at Montigny where their escort from 1 Squadron lost an SE5 to Jasta 42. Closer to the battlefront, around 1000hrs, 84 Squadron launched a successful mission to destroy the German observation balloons around Villers Outreaux despite the protection provided by Jasta 46, while further south, a large formation of British fighters tangled with Jasta 22 over Montbrehain.

At 1030hrs Debeney's French 1e Armée launched into the fray as the troops of 31e and 8e Corps assaulted Urvillers and Cerizy close behind their artillery barrage. By 1130hrs 169e and 152e Divisions had captured Urvillers, with 500 prisoners of the 6 Bayerische and 231. Infanterie-Divisions in XXVI Reservekorps. Further south, 60e Division captured Cerizy from 208. Infanterie-Division. However, the initial success of these attacks could not be maintained. When the French infantry attempted to push east of the trenches lining the St Quentin–La Fere road, they could not overcome the heavy machine-gun fire which blocked their way. By early afternoon the attack had stalled.

As the extent of the crisis enveloping 2. Infanterie- and 79. Reserve-Divisions at Bellenglise became clear, Endres prepared to protect the right flank of his corps and the junction between 2. and 18. Armees. At 1100hrs elements of 11. Infanterie-Division in Bohain and Fresnoy were prepared for action later in the day, while 25. Reserve-Division in Lesdins and 221. Infanterie-Division in Séboncourt were also brought to higher readiness. In the Australian Corps, the staff of 3rd Australian Division picked through the situation reports coming back from their brigades in an effort to re-invigorate the stalled attack. The growing realization that they were facing a relatively intact defensive system prompted the obvious suggestion that it could be turned by a flanking movement through 5th Australian Division's sector to the south. At corps headquarters, however, Brig. Blamey, the Chief of Staff, remained unconvinced, citing other reports that 27th (US) Division troops were still ahead of them, and ordered the attack to be re-started as planned from the west. Consequently, when 10th Brigade attempted to move forwards south of Gillemont Farm around 1500hrs it was quickly brought to a halt by heavy fire from the field guns, machine guns and trench mortars

German 76mm trench mortar team. This image is posed but it gives a good impression of a firing post dug into a trench line. (IWM, Q55018)

of 121. Infanterie-Division, now reinforced by Infanterie-Regiment 87. Meanwhile, although 11th Brigade was able to clear the Main Hindenburg Line trenches northwards up to the Bony–Bellicourt road in bitter fighting, its attempts to push east from the Tunnel Mound withered under a hail of fire from German positions of 185. Infanterie-Division, now being reinforced by the regiments of 2. Garde-Division coming into line from the east. Likewise around Nauroy, as 5th Australian Division consolidated its positions and waited for the situation in front of 3rd Australian Division to improve, its forward troops noted

the arrival of the leading elements of 21. Infanterie-Division now deploying between Joncourt and Estrées to the east.

Despite the confusion and setbacks being suffered by the Australians and Americans, IX Corps' attack continued the success of the early morning. At 1120hrs the protective barrage placed east of Bellenglise moved forwards once again as the assault recommenced. Although 139th Brigade on the right of 46th Division had the more complex defences to clear along the north bank of the canal, it was now cutting across the boundary between 2. Armee and 18. Armee, driving into the rear right flank of 79. Reserve-Division to the south. As the fog began to clear, however, a battery from Reserve-Feld-Artillerie-Regiment 63, supporting 79. Reserve-Division, was able to fire across the canal and destroyed the tanks now supporting the British. As the attack stuttered, infantry from 6th Sherwood Foresters crossed the canal, cleared the battery position with the bayonet and drove off the supporting infantry. Having dealt with this threat from the right flank, the advance towards Lehaucourt recommenced and the village was cleared. On the left, 138th Brigade advanced over open ground towards Magny-la-Fosse, clearing the shattered remnants of 2. Infanterie-Division withdrawing ahead of them. The tanks operating in support were able to clear paths through the wire that was otherwise unscathed by the barrage, and by 1315hrs, 5th Lincolns had breached the Hindenburg Support Line to secure the village. 5th Leicesters took over the advance at 1340hrs and by 1500hrs were digging in on the final objective and establishing contact with the Australians on their left and 139th Brigade on their right. As the divisional historian noted, as far as the eye could see, British troops were advancing.

Fourth Army's attack east of Bellenglise in the afternoon now presented a critical threat to Endres, as a 'yawning gap' began to appear between the beleaguered elements of 79. Reserve- and 11. Infanterie-Divisions – who were trying to concentrate around the Le Tronquoy Tunnel – and those of 2. Infanterie-Division, which were moving back towards Magny-la-Fosse. However, with XXVI and XVIII Reservekorps having successfully contained the French attack at Urvillers, he was now able to concentrate on his right flank without the risk of Hutier demanding reserves for employment elsewhere. At 1200hrs, the remainder of 11. Infanterie-Division was ordered to reinforce 79. Reserve-Division at Fontaine-Uterte, while 25. Reserve-Division was directed to concentrate around Lesdins. At 1550hrs, as the British assault continued to drive deeper into the defences, Endres ordered 221. Infanterie-Division forward to secure the junction with 2. Armee north of the Bellenglise–Sequehart road.

As Endres deployed his reserves, Braithwaite's IX Corps prepared to exploit their successful 'break in'. By 1530hrs, as 46th Division reached its objectives, the brigades of 32nd Division were already moving through Bellenglise in order to take over the battle. By 1730hrs they were in their assault positions, and at 1800hrs, they advanced as the artillery commenced the covering barrage. On the right, 14th Brigade headed towards the Le Tronquoy Tunnel and by nightfall had seized its northern entrance from the shattered elements

Trenches around the Le Tronquoy Tunnel. The British 32nd Division advanced from left to right late in the evening of 29 September. They halted under fire from 11. Infanterie-Division deployed between the tunnel and Levergies. (IWM, Q55622)

'ROASTING SAUSAGES – FLAMING ONIONS' (PP. 58–59)

Throughout World War I, the contest between aircraft, observation balloons and the forces that protected them provided some of the most dramatic and dangerous aerial combat. By late 1918 the Luftstreikräfte had 182 balloon sections (*Ballonzüge*) each of which the 'AE' Type could operate at an altitude of 5,000ft.

The balloons themselves quickly became intoxicating targets for the more ambitious and daredevil fighter pilots. They were notoriously difficult to destroy as their hydrogen contents would only ignite if hit with Buckingham tracer ammunition at close range – an almost suicidal 50 yards being the RAF recommendation. Each balloon was usually heavily defended, being surrounded by anti-aircraft units deploying heavy machine guns and potentially protected by flights of fighters. The bursts of greenish-white tracer fired by the 20mm and 37mm cannon were nicknamed 'flaming onions' by the Allied aircrews, following the optical illusion that they were 'strung' together.

Such difficult targets required specialized tactics such as those used by the RAF in 1918. Each mission was flown in squadron strength, with one flight providing the balloon striking force and the other two flights providing protection from German fighters at higher levels.

The destruction of the German observation balloons was a critical part of the RAF's mission on 29 September, and the specialists of 84 Squadron equipped with SE5a aircraft were one of the squadrons entrusted with this task. Fifteen aircraft took off at 0945hrs and headed for the area around Beaurevoir with 'A' Flight, under command of 2Lt. Sidney Highwood (1), designated as the balloon striking force.

As soon as I reached the lines I could see Fokker biplanes above me, but as I had 'B' and 'C' Flights just above me I decided I would have a dive at the balloons. As soon as the Fokkers saw me dive, they immediately dived at my flight, but Capt. Falkenburg immediately engaged them, sending one down in flames and the remainder were forced down.

We carried on straight for the balloons. 2Lt. Rees and myself sent one down in flames, and then seeing another one to the south east, I dived on it getting a good burst into it from very close range, it also went down in flames (2).

By this time about 20 Fokkers had collected, but as soon as they tried to attack us they were driven away by the flights above. The whole time we were across the lines the two flights above were fighting with the Fokkers as they attacked us.

Combat Report, 2Lt. S. W. Highwood 29 September 1918

84 Squadron was credited with four balloons destroyed on this sortie; however, Highwood's belief that the Fokkers had been held off proved to be false. Amongst the aircraft from Jasta 46 was Vizefeldwebel Oskar Hennrich, himself a balloon-busting ace. Acting on this day as 'poacher turned gamekeeper', he was credited with shooting down Highwood's wingman, 2Lt. D. C. Rees (KIA).

Somewhat surprisingly given their penchant for attacking balloons, both Highwood (16 victories including nine balloons) and Hennrich (20 victories including 13 balloons) survived the war.

of 79. Reserve-Division. On the left, however, 97th Brigade headed towards Levergies but was unable to dislodge the patchwork force, consisting of five battalions from 11. Infanterie-Division, who had reached this point earlier in the afternoon. As the defences now began to thicken, and being far ahead of the units to their left and right, 32nd Division formed defensive flanks and prepared to consolidate their position overnight.

In the evening, as the fighting died down on the IX Corps' front, 6th Division began to hand over its positions to the incoming 47e Division of the French 15e Corps, with the relief being completed overnight. As the tired British withdrew into IX Corps rear areas, Debeney's men prepared to enter the fray the following day.

In the Australian Corps, Monash and his staff spent the late afternoon reassessing the situation facing their stalled left flank. Having seen the afternoon attacks fail, at 1605hrs he ordered 9th Brigade to redeploy from the rear left of 3rd Australian Division to 5th Australian Division's sector and attack the Hindenburg Line from the right flank. Here they would attack northwards to clear the Hindenburg Line in conjunction with 15th Brigade, the reserve of the 5th Australian Division. The attack was scheduled for 0600hrs the following day. However, as the troops began their 12km approach march, rain began to fall, and in the deteriorating conditions it became apparent that they would not arrive in time for the assault. Ingeniously, 5th Australian Division's commander, Maj. Gen. Gellibrand, ordered 11th Brigade, which was already in position, to take over the task, with 42nd and 43rd Battalions instructed to clear the Main Hindenburg Line and 41st Battalion to clear the Advanced Hindenburg Line. As 9th Brigade swung behind 11th Brigade, 33rd and 35th Battalions in the lead would link up with the 42nd and 43rd, while the 34th Battalion in the rear would link up with the 41st. This rapid redeployment and regrouping was a hallmark of the Australian Corps' operations throughout the final campaigns of the war and highlighted the flexible and effective staff work their headquarters could produce.

However, the one problem that would carry over into the next day was the inability to deploy the full weight of artillery support. The aerial reconnaissance reports of American troops in isolated pockets beyond the Main Hindenburg Line continued to preclude the use of heavy artillery. A compromise was reached with Maj. Gen. O'Ryan, that field artillery could be used on the Hindenburg Main Line as it was demonstrably still in German possession, but the ability to suppress German artillery and machine guns in depth was severely compromised.

Meanwhile, the boundary between 2. Armee and 17. Armee continued to give the Germans concern. With XIV Reservekorps and 54. Generalkommando now facing deep penetrations of the Hindenburg Line to their left at St Quentin and right at Cambrai, Morgen and Larisch had little hesitation in ordering an overnight withdrawal back towards the canal line. This sector was to be reinforced by 206. Infanterie-Division, which was withdrawn from 18. Armee at St Quentin and prepared for transfer to 17. Armee at Cambrai. Meanwhile 3. Landwehr-Division was ordered north to Flanders from Guise. As a result of these transfers, 18. Armee was forced to issue warning orders to 241. Infanterie-Division to be transferred to I Bayerische Armeekorps immediately after it was relieved from its front-line positions in XVIII Reservekorps by the incoming 232. Infanterie-Division.

At 2345hrs Rawlinson issued orders for his army's operations the following day. IX Corps was to secure the whole of the Tronquoy Tunnel to assist the French, before swinging north-east to secure the ridge between Sequehart and Ramicourt. On the left it was to capture Joncourt to assist the Australian advance further north. The Australian Corps was to relieve the Americans still believed to be in front of it and secure the rest of the Main Hindenburg Line as far as Vendhuille and the Hindenburg Support Line as far as Gouy. The American Corps was to withdraw once relieved. III Corps was to secure Vendhuille if the opportunity arose. XIII Corps and the Cavalry Corps were held in reserve.

While the battle raged between Cambrai and St Quentin, events no less dramatic were unfolding at OHL in the Hotel Britannique in Spa. At 1000hrs, as 46th Division was clearing Bellenglise, Ludendorff and Hindenburg outlined the crisis now enveloping the army to the Kaiser and stated the urgent need for an armistice to allow their troops to regroup. The Foreign Minister, Admiral von Hintze, suggested that a 'revolution from above' be implemented and an approach be made to President Wilson for a cessation of hostilities based on his 'Fourteen Point' speech. It was hoped that the empowerment of the more radical socialist parties in the Reichstag would distract their attention from the shock of defeat in the field and potentially position them to take some of the blame. The Kaiser gave his consent, but the Chancellor, Hertling, resigned at the prospect. His post was offered to the liberal Prinz Max of Baden to see how much of Imperial Germany's crumbling edifice could be saved.

'THE SUPPLY OF OHL RESERVES CAN NO LONGER BE ASSUMED', 30 SEPTEMBER

Although the German leadership was now seeking an armistice, the initial assaults of the General Offensive were beginning to stall. In the Meuse-Argonne, the French 4e Armée attacked again, but made only a limited advance of around 2–3km and were completely blocked by a strong German defence west of Somme-Py. A similar situation was unfolding in Flanders, where heavy rain fell onto the shattered battlefields making administration of the attacking armies almost impossible. To make matters worse, the six German divisions deployed from reserve were now in place to augment the defences. The GAF advanced 2–3km towards the north-west but on a narrowing front as their flanks were held at Dixmude in the west, and against the old 1917 Flanders II defence line south-east of Passchendaele. The left of the British Second Army also stalled in this sector, but closed up to the Lys further south. In order to overcome the mounting logistic difficulties, Second Army withdrew two infantry brigades of the 14th Division and sent them back to clear the increasingly mud-clogged roads. It was up to the BEF on the Hindenburg Line to maintain the momentum.

Troops of the British Second Army struggling forwards along the devastated roads in Flanders. (IWM, Q11763)

'The battalion beat off the ninth attack in two days' – the battle of the Canal du Nord

Overnight, General Horne ordered First Army to continue its attempts to cross the Schelde Canal north of Cambrai, and Gen. Currie planned a two-phase assault. 1st, 3rd and 4th Canadian Divisions were to seize the crossings at Ramillies and Eswars, before 1st Canadian and 11th British Divisions struck north to capture Abancourt and Fressies. The first phase was launched at 0600hrs but was in trouble from the outset. The smokescreen planned to shield 4th Canadian Division from the flanking positions of 22. Infanterie-Division on the high ground east of Abancourt did not materialize. As a result, when 11th Brigade pushed forwards it suffered heavy casualties from this direction, including most of its officers and NCOs, and remained fixed on the railway line east of Blécourt. It was the ninth attack faced by Infanterie-Regiment 83 in two days. Further south, 3rd Canadian Division had better luck, as 7th Brigade pushed 207. Infanterie-Division back through Tilloy. However, the failure of 4th Canadian Division exposed its left flank to fire from the German posts at Blécourt and they could not move further east. As the first phase of Currie's plan had failed, the second phase of the attack was cancelled.

In Third Army, Gen. Byng's orders also directed his southern two corps to drive on to the Schelde Canal, but the German withdrawal in the night disrupted their efforts. Harper's IV Corps moved early at 0300hrs, when the New Zealand Division patrols detected the German withdrawal. 1st and 2nd New Zealand Brigades moved forwards at once but found the bridge at Vaucelles destroyed and the western approaches to the canal swept by fire from the eastern bank. 1st New Zealand Brigade managed to cross to an island in the canal at Crèvecour, but could go no further. 5th Division advanced behind a barrage at 0400hrs, catching the rearguards of the Jäger and 21. Reserve-Divisions as they pulled back. However, with the main German force now occupying the high ground overlooking the canal from the east, the British were unable to enter Banteux. A small party infiltrated across the canal north of the village, but as the Germans moved forwards to outflank them, they were withdrawn. V Corps did not detect the absence of 54. Generalkommado until 0800hrs. When patrols of 33rd and 21st Divisions followed up, they found that Larisch's men had crossed safely to the eastern bank and now dominated the canal from the heights between Bantouzelle and Honnecourt.

Closer to Cambrai, Haldane's VI Corps attempted to develop the bridgehead seized the previous day. 2nd Division tried to secure the high ground north of Rumilly at 0500hrs, but they were repulsed by heavy machine-gun fire from 18 Reserve-Division. At 0630hrs, 62nd Division attacked between Rumilly and Crèvecoeur without any artillery barrage, but made little headway against the tiring 6. and 113. Infanterie-Divisions. Another assault at 1230hrs, this time with artillery support, entered Rumilly but was ejected by German counter-attacks. Other minor gains were withdrawn to enable a much stronger barrage to be planned for the next day. Fergusson's XVII Corps faced much stronger opposition when it tried to clear the southern suburbs of Cambrai at 0630hrs. Heavy machine-gun fire from 18. Reserve- and 3. Marine-Divisions pinned 57th and 63rd Divisions to their line of departure. A further attempt at 1230hrs fared little better, although 57th Division was able to clear Proville.

The day's fighting around Cambrai represented a relative success for the Germans in their efforts to stave off disaster. Both Etzel's XVIII Armeekorps and Morgen's XIV Reservekorps had bought badly needed time for Rupprecht, Boehn and their colleagues commanding the corps to the north and south. But their troops were rapidly tiring, and there was little hope for significant reinforcement.

Flank attack at Bony – the battle of the St Quentin Canal

In Fourth Army, the Australian Corps was the first to advance when, at 0600hrs, patrols of 10th Brigade found the Hindenburg Outpost Line had been evacuated overnight and quickly occupied the trenches. Further east, despite the limited artillery support, 14th Australian Brigade punched into the left flank of 2. Garde-Division and drove it back up the Hindenburg Support Line in furious trench fighting. Attack and counter-attack flowed back and forth before the Australian advance was brought to a halt after 1,000m.

11th Australian Brigade's assault along the Main Hindenburg Line did not go smoothly. The delivery of orders and reorganization of the forward troops proved extremely difficult overnight in deteriorating weather conditions, and the infantry were not ready or in position at 0600hrs. The seven tanks available to support them set off alone and drove to Bony machine-gunning the defenders as they went. Coming under heavy fire from Bony itself, they returned and went to the rear. As the infantry got into position, the fire now sweeping across the open ground forced the attack into the trenches. The mixed force of battalions from 9th and 11th Australian Brigades then moved forwards with bayonet and bomb against the right flank of 2. Garde-Division, but after advancing around 500m it was brought to a halt around mid-afternoon by the weight of fire now being directed at it from Bony.

On the Australians' left, III Corps' early-morning patrols also detected the German withdrawal back over the canal to the Main Hindenburg Line at Vendhuille. By 1000hrs 18th Division had its foremost troops in the village, but it wasn't secured until 1545hrs, after which time posts were established along the canal. 12th Division secured the boundary with V Corps in Third Army to the north before being relieved by 18th Division and withdrawn from the front line.

At the junction of the Australian and IX Corps, efforts to advance towards Estrées and Joncourt met stiff resistance. Patrols from 15th Australian Brigade attempted to infiltrate the forward positions of 21. Infanterie-Division in the early morning but were beaten back by intense machine-gun fire. On the left of IX Corps, 96th Brigade cleared the remnants of 75. Reserve- and 2. Infanterie-Divisions from positions west of Joncourt, while artillery was prepared for a coordinated attack on the village later in the day. Further south, 14th Brigade cleared Le Tronquoy village and the tunnel by 1145hrs. From this position, it was able to assist the advance of 1st Division by engaging the right flank and rear of 197. Infanterie-Division defending Thoringy and Talana Hill. As the Germans

Concrete barrier inside the southern entrance of the Bellicourt Tunnel. This was cleared by Australian engineers on 30 September as the battle raged above them. (IWM, E(AUS) 3598)

pulled back, 1st and 32nd Divisions were able to link up at Le Tronquoy. At 1430hrs, 96th Brigade assaulted Joncourt but was unable to keep up with its covering barrage and was drawn into a bitter struggle with 21. Infanterie-Division. Although it established itself in the southern part of the village, it could not secure it. At Levergies, 11. Infanterie-Division was reinforced by 241. Infanterie-Division now arriving into line. They held off 97th Brigade until 1830hrs, when a concentrated British artillery bombardment finally helped overcome resistance. As night fell, IX Corps held the line from Le Tronquoy to Joncourt and prepared to drive towards Sequehart and Ramicourt the next day.

A German officer of Infanterie-Regiment 87, captured by the Australians in the fighting around Joncourt. (IWM, E(AUS) 3403)

Having relieved IX Corps the previous night, Gén. de Fonclare's 15e Corps finally began its drive around the north of St Quentin. At 1700hrs, 47e Division advanced behind a creeping barrage, but made limited headway against heavy machine-gun fire from 197. Infanterie- and 82. Reserve-Divisions. By nightfall they had not reached the St Quentin–Bellicourt road, still some 3km south-west of Le Tronquoy. Earlier, 31e Corps and 8e Corps attempted to continue their attacks at Urvillers and Cerizy. However, both 152e and 169e Divisions were unable to overcome the machine guns and artillery of Watter's XXVI Armeekorps, and minimal gains were made west of Urvillers. The same situation affected 60e Division in 8e Corps, which continued to be held up east of Cerizy. The limited gains made by Debeney's French 1re Armée caused an irritated Haig to send a note to Foch requesting his assistance to urge them forward.

Notwithstanding this dispute, the cumulative effect of the General Offensive continued to deliver results, as the relentless pressure on resources began to crack the German Army. Hindenburg had already noted that the *Eingrief* divisions were now mostly plugging gaps that were appearing in the line rather than delivering the counter-attacks for which they were intended. Of greater consequence, however, was the recognition that without sufficient reserves, prolonged resistance by the front-line troops in untenable positions was pointless. OHL therefore authorized controlled tactical withdrawals where the situation demanded, with the intent that casualties would continue to be inflicted on the Allies, and that time be bought to withdraw essential equipment, destroy communications and prepare the Hermann-Lys position as a permanent defence line. Additionally, preparations commenced for another defence line further to the rear from Antwerp, through Charleroi to the Meuse. Critically, the *Heeresgruppen* were warned that they could no longer expect further reserves from OHL.

Rupprecht immediately issued orders for 6. Armee and 17. Armee to fall back to the Haute Deule and Sensée canals between Armentières and Douai. To the south, Hutier ordered 18. Armee to evacuate St Quentin and withdraw behind the Somme to the east of the city. In 2. Armee, IV Reservekorps and 51. Generalkommando were ordered to withdraw to the Hindenburg Reserve Line south of Estrées and to form a link from there to the Hindenburg Support Line at Le Catelet. Overnight, 54. Infanterie-Division moved to Le Catelet-Gouy, 2. Garde- and 119. Infanterie-Divisions linked the two lines west of Beaurevoir, 21. Infanterie-Division held Estrées and 241. Infanterie-Division held Joncourt. Further south, 1. Reserve-Division relieved 208. Infanterie-Division, which was immediately warned for transfer to 17. Armee at Cambrai.

'CASUALTIES AMONGST THE LEADERS WERE HUGE', 1 OCTOBER

As the Germans desperately pulled back their most exposed forces, the Allies fought to keep the pressure on them. In the Argonne, 4e Armée continued its attempts to drive the German 3. Armee from its last positions south of the river Aisne, but as with the previous days, the German rearguard action remained effective. The French advanced approximately 4km and seized the high ground south of Grandpré but could not reach the river. At Vouziers they moved forwards 3km, but strong counter-attacks drove them back. At Ypres the weather improved, but there was only limited activity as the British Second Army reorganized its positions and carried out some minor attacks. At 1630hrs, GAF ordered a night assault to break through the German line, but the British were unable to comply. In the evening, Second Army was informed that the Franco-Belgian resupply system had broken down, and in response II Brigade RAF was tasked to deliver rations by air the next day. This loss of momentum was mirrored on the Hindenburg Line, where fatigue and extended lines of communication began to impede Haig's armies.

Horne closes the battle – the battle of the Canal du Nord
At Cambrai, Currie's plan remained the same as the previous day, with 3rd Canadian Division seizing Pont d'Aire and Ramillies, 4th Canadian Division seizing the crossing at Eswars, and 1st Canadian Division securing Blécourt, Cuvillers, Bantigny and Abancourt. 11th British Division was to secure the flank, while 2nd Canadian Division and the Canadian Independent Force was to pass through 3rd Canadian Division if the canal was crossed.

The attack was launched at 0500hrs behind a creeping barrage 6km wide from Neuville to Épinoy. This presaged a day of extremely heavy artillery support, with the Canadian Corps firing 7,000 tons of ammunition. By 0700hrs, both 9th Canadian Brigade in 3rd Canadian Division, and 11th Canadian Brigade in 4th Canadian Division had reached the Blécourt road and were preparing to sweep down on the river and canal crossing points. As they did so, heavy machine-gun and artillery fire from 26. Reserve-Division raked across the forward slope on which they were exposed and they were soon forced to draw back. In 1st Canadian Division, 3rd Canadian Brigade quickly drove the tired troops of 22. Infanterie-Division back through Blécourt and was east of Cuvillers and Bantigny by 0800hrs. On their left, however, 1st Canadian Brigade had been unable to secure Abancourt – despite inflicting high officer and JNCO casualties on 35. Infanterie-Division – and the German artillery on the high ground behind the village was soon turned on 3rd Canadian Brigade to the south. By 1000hrs, 3rd Canadian Brigade had withdrawn to Blécourt before a counter-attack by a combined force of 234. and 220. Infanterie-Divisions drove them back out of the village. Without heavy artillery to dominate the key ground at Abancourt, there would be no advance in this sector. 11th Division's attack stalled on new wire obstacles until 1400hrs, when reinforcements arrived. Although an attack at

The battles of the St Quentin Canal and the Beaurevoir Line

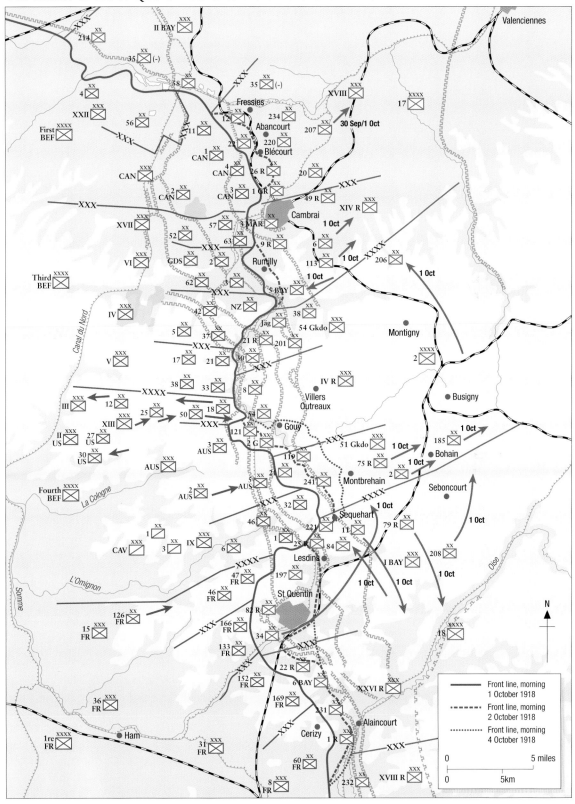

View across Bantigny Ravine from the south. Bantigny is to the left. Infantry from 3rd Canadian Brigade advanced from left to right down the ravine and across the spur in the near ground. They were forced back by artillery and machine-gun fire from 22. Infanterie-Division positions on the far spur. (Author)

1530hrs failed, at 1830hrs a third assault managed to link up with the Canadian left flank before finally settling down for the night. After five days' hard fighting Horne halted further attacks from Currie's men until further notice.

South of Cambrai, IV and VI Corps worked hard to expand their bridgehead over the Schelde Canal. At 0600hrs the New Zealand Division crossed the canal at Masnières before swinging right to capture Crèvecour from the west. Counter-attacks from 5. Bayerische-Infanterie-Division were fought off, but the Kiwis sustained severe casualties. In VI Corps, Haldane ordered 2nd and 3rd Divisions to capture Rumilly at 0600hrs from a mixed force from 3. Marine- and 9. Reserve-Divisions. Limited headway was made during the morning, as coordination with the artillery proved difficult. The Germans took full advantage to infiltrate troops back into position after the barrage had passed. Only in the evening was a new assault organized which surprised the defenders and captured the village.

By the close of the day, Byng's men had secured a bridgehead from Crèvecour, through Rumilly to Proville, but they badly needed a period to recuperate. Furthermore, although XVII and VI Corps were well positioned to threaten Cambrai from the west and south, IV and V Corps were held in front of the canal and the Hindenburg Line defences from Crèvecour to the boundary with Fourth Army at Le Catelet. As such the battle of the Canal du Nord was closed down while the troops were resupplied and the heavy artillery brought forward.

The cavalry moves up – the battle of the St Quentin Canal

In Fourth Army, Rawlinson intended to breach the Hindenburg Reserve Line and clear a passage for the cavalry to drive into the open country to the east. This task was given to IX and Australian Corps while XIII Corps relieved III Corps. In addition to clearing the way for the cavalry, the attack was to threaten the German defences facing the right of Third Army from the south.

As the rain continued through the night, Monash was persuaded by Gellibrand to continue to exploit the successful operations on the right flank of his corps. 5th Australian Division moved into its assaulting positions to clear the ridge between Joncourt and the forward troops of the 3rd Australian Division in the Hindenburg Support Line south-east of Bony. 2nd Australian Division would then push through to attack the Hindenburg Reserve Line if the opportunity arose.

At 0600hrs an accurate barrage opened the attack, and by 0800hrs the Australian infantry had reached Joncourt and the eastern edge of Estrées. They were joined at Joncourt by 32nd Division and together they occupied the village. At 0900hrs, 14th Australian Brigade secured Estrées but was blocked by heavy artillery fire from 21. Infanterie-Division as it attempted to cross the exposed slopes of Mill

German trenches in front of Joncourt. Note the rifle pits that have been dug along the Hindenburg Support Line, which appears only to have been marked out at this point. (IWM, Q9816)

Ridge and advance further east. As 5th Australian Division cleared Estrées, 3rd Australian Division continued its attacks northwards towards Bony. At 0200hrs, patrols discovered the absence of German troops in the Main Hindenburg Line and by 0945hrs troops of 10th and 11th Brigades were infiltrating into Bony. However, they halted as they tried to push further north, when sharp machine-gun and artillery fire from 54. Infanterie-Division in Le Catelet and Gouy indicated the new position of the German front line.

A German ammunition train destroyed in an air raid. Each division needed over 40 trains to move. The destruction of rolling stock and the blockage of key junctions had a paralysing effect on the German ability to move troops around the front. (IWM, Q87612)

Having cleared Joncourt with the Australians, 32nd Division organized a further assault on the Hindenburg Reserve Line between Ramicourt and Sequehart for 1600hrs. Throughout the afternoon a heavy artillery bombardment pounded the German trenches until the infantry moved off. Advancing behind a creeping barrage, 5th/6th Royal Scots drove 221. Infanterie-Division out of Sequehart, but converging counter-attacks at 2030hrs – led personally by the German Commander, GenMaj. von Chevallerie – forced them back to the western edge of the village. However, 32nd Division's main attack, delivered by 96th and 97th Brigades, succeeded in breaking into the Hindenburg Reserve Line in front of Ramicourt. Nine tanks played an essential role by breaking down the strong wire obstacles, after which the infantry from the Border and Manchester Regiments soon cleared a 1,400m stretch of trenches, taking over 200 prisoners from Infanterie-Regiment 473. 32nd Division then attempted to pass its small cavalry detachment through the gap but they were blocked by machine-gun fire from Ramicourt. Nor were the Germans minded to accept the loss of their last trench line in this sector, as 241. Infanterie-Division's reserve battalions counter-attacked throughout the night, but the British held their gains.

While the Australian and IX Corps continued their operations east of the canal, Lt. Gen. Morland's XIII Corps relieved the exhausted III Corps at Vendhuille, with 50th Division entering the line in place of 18th Division.

In the air, the clearing weather allowed the RAF to re-enter the fray after two days of relative inactivity. At 0615hrs, 22 DH9 and DH4 bombers of IX Brigade RAF took off to attack the rail junction at Aulnoye, 40km east of Cambrai. Although seven were compelled to turn back with engine trouble, 26 112lb bombs were dropped on the target. At 0800hrs a second wave of 29 bombers was dispatched to the same target. This time 16 turned back and the remainder were pounced upon by German fighters as they crossed the front line. They ditched their bombs and aborted the mission. More successful attacks were launched in the afternoon, when ten DH9s bombed Aulnoy and destroyed an ammunition train. The attacks at Aulnoy continued into the night, with 207 Squadron's Handley Page aircraft, while 102 Squadron from III Brigade RAF ignited trains at Bertry and Beaurevoir.

In 1re Armée, 15e Corps prepared to envelop St Quentin from the north-west, with 47e Division attacking Lesdins and 46e Division attacking Omissy at 0900hrs. Progress was slow despite strong artillery support, as 197. and 82. Reserve-Divisions put up stout resistance with machine-gun and artillery fire. When the fighting calmed down around 1630hrs, neither French objective had been taken, with 15e Corps having suffered 12 men killed and 96 wounded during the day. The French command's conservative instructions were being followed to the letter. 36e Corps pushed towards St Quentin from the west and had established footholds in Faubourg d'Isle on the south of the city, with patrols penetrating to the bridge at Rouvroy when the advance was halted.

With the left flank of his corps now secure behind the St Quentin Canal, Endres now turned his attention to the increasingly dangerous situation on his right at Sequehart and Ramicourt. In order to bolster the overstretched troops on the boundary between 2. and 18. Armees, he ordered 34. Infanterie-Division to deploy at Sequehart, while exchanging the exhausted 11. Infanterie-Division for 24. Infanterie-Division in Gontard's XIV Armeekorps which was directed to Ramicourt.

While the Allied armies continued to grind their way through the German forces on the Hindenburg Line, the political developments in Germany precipitated by the conference at Spa two days earlier now began to gather pace. As doubts grew over Prinz Max of Baden's will to form a government, Ludendorff issued an ultimatum to his liaison officer in the Reichstag, Major von Bussche. If no government agreement could be guaranteed, OHL would send the declaration to the Allied powers come what may. Bussche took his brief and prepared to meet the politicians at 0900hrs the following day.

THE BREAKTHROUGH IS DENIED, 2 OCTOBER

With the British attack at Cambrai paused, attempts by the GAF to advance in Flanders achieved little in the face of determined resistance. Unable to bring heavy artillery forward, the Allies could not suppress the machine-gun and artillery fire of 4. Armee. Given the tactical situation, the operation was closed down until the GAF could bring forwards its artillery and improve supply routes across the shattered Flanders terrain. Meanwhile, the two remaining operations both readied their cavalry to break through the German lines. In the Argonne orders were issued to advance towards Rethel, with 1er Corps de Cavalerie positioned to support should the German line be broken through. Success, however, remained elusive with minor gains of around 1.5–2km being made, but the German defence held after hard fighting. With the German line intact, the cavalry was stood down. At midday, orders were given for the attack to continue the next day with the same objectives.

Rawlinson cuts his losses – the battle of the St Quentin Canal

Overnight, Rawlinson issued orders to continue the attempt to launch a cavalry breakthrough towards Fresnoy. However, rather than advancing towards the east, Fourth Army spent much of the day fighting off determined counter-attacks from 2. Armee and 18. Armee. The day saw almost no activity on the Australian Corps front as 50th Division sideslipped right to relieve 3rd Australian Division, while 2nd Australian Division relieved 5th Australian Division.

In IX Corps, at 0730hrs 32nd Division broke into Sequehart once more with support from the aircraft of V and IX Brigades RAF. But for a second time, the energetic efforts of GenMaj. von Chevallerie restored the situation as he led his troops to recapture the lost position at 0900hrs. Further north, at 0830hrs, 96th and 97th Brigades' attempt to push forward through

Ramicourt were thwarted by heavy fire from their front and left flank. No ground was gained, and as a result at 1115hrs the Cavalry Corps was stood down.

The strengthening German defence and the weakening British attack caused Rawlinson to postpone further operations until a more thoroughly prepared assault could be launched. This decision closed the battle of the St Quentin Canal, and the battle of the Beaurevoir Line began.

East and south of St Quentin, Debeney's men had little success. At 0600hrs, 15e Corps' 47e and 46e Divisions attempted to seize Lesdins and Morcourt

Itancourt from the north. The Hindenburg Line ran parallel to the road through the fields to the left before turning right to enclose the northern and western edges of the village. At 1530hrs on 2 October 1918, 169e Division broke into the forward trenches before 231. Infanterie-Division restored the line with a counter-attack. (Author)

respectively. Neither made much headway against the alert German defences. A small bridgehead was established at Morcourt but a vigorous counter-attack by 197. Infanterie- and 82. Reserve-Divisions in the early afternoon threw them back across the canal. Likewise, 36e Corps was unable to cross the canal at St Quentin, while 31e Corps was pushed back to their starting positions after briefly entering the Hindenburg Line at Itancourt.

While the fighting on the Western Front moved towards a pause, OHL's bombshell was launched into the unsuspecting political arena. In Berlin at 0900hrs Maj. von Bussche informed the stunned Reichstag party leaders that while the defensive battle was being successfully fought, the lack of reserves and Allied tanks meant that the war was lost. Meanwhile, at the Imperial Conference in Spa, Prinz Max prevaricated over the request for an immediate armistice on the grounds that it would disclose Germany's weak negotiating position. Hindenburg and Ludendorff stood firm over the issue and the Kaiser informed Prinz Max that he must support OHL. Having demanded written confirmation from Hindenburg that the armistice was essential, Prinz Max began the drafting process in earnest.

NO RESPITE, 3 OCTOBER

While the German politicians tried to digest OHL's stark admission, the Allies kept the pressure up where they could, and worked feverishly to get their armies back in the fight. This proved harder than expected in the Argonne, where a German counter-attack drove the French out of Challerange, preventing any offensive action there later in the day. At 0550hrs the renewed attempt to clear the way for the cavalry breached the German first line on Blanc Mont and at Orfeuil, but the objective on Notre Dames des Champs remained in German hands. Further attacks were made at 1600hrs, but there was no breakthrough. With no gap to exploit, the Cavalry Corps was stood down once more. 4e Armée reported to Pétain that it was now in dire need of fresh troops before it could renew its advance. Although these were forthcoming, they were not immediately available and, consequently, the battle reached an operational pause.

'The enemy fought stoutly' – the battle of the Beaurevoir Line

Rawlinson's orders for the new attack were succinct and to the point. The Australian and IX Corps were to attack together and breach the Hindenburg

The Hindenburg Reserve Line. Although the wire was in position, the line of this trench had only been marked out rather than being fully excavated. (IWM, E(AUS) 3957)

Reserve Line between Beaurevoir and Sequehart. XIII Corps was to form a defensive flank facing north, while the Cavalry Corps was be held at 60 minutes' notice to move from 0900hrs in readiness to exploit the expected breakthrough. The French 1re Armée was to continue its support on the right. Facing them, the troops of 2. and 18. Armees were under orders to hold their last line of defence at all costs, to protect the critical rail junction at Busigny and prevent the encirclement of Cambrai from the south. As the British troops moved into position overnight, a heavy fog formed to cloak their assembly positions. The main assault was to be delivered by IX Corps, which had brought 46th Division back into the line for the purpose. 32nd Division and 1st Division were to support on the right. The Australian assault was to be delivered by 2nd Australian Division, with 50th Division covering their left.

At 0605hrs the attack opened as the barrage crashed down on the German defences. In 46th Division, 139th Brigade advanced towards Ramicourt and Montbrehain. Twelve supporting tanks quickly flattened lanes through the thick wire for the infantry, and by 0730hrs Ramicourt had been secured. To the south, 137th Brigade had more difficulty and had to clear Infanterie-Regiment 473 from its concrete emplacements and supporting artillery positions at bayonet point. By 0800hrs it had done so, but at heavy cost, prompting their historian to remark on the tenacity of the German troops. At Sequehart, 221. Infanterie-Division was in the process of being relieved by 34. Infanterie-Division when Lambert's 32nd Division struck. While 97th Brigade outflanked the village from the north, 14th Brigade attacked from the west. By 0625hrs they had secured a line to the east of the village but an immediate counter-attack soon drove them back. However, Lambert's men reorganized and renewed their efforts. By 0800hrs Sequehart was back in British hands. On the Australian front, 5th and 7th Australian Brigades stormed into the forward positions of 21. and 119. Infanterie-Divisions. By 0745hrs, 5th Australian Brigade had cleared both trenches of the Hindenburg Reserve Line, with 7th Australian Brigade completing the same task by 0800hrs. Attempts to advance further were blocked by heavy fire from the higher ground to the east and north, and the forward troops noted the ominous sight of German troops massing for a counter-attack. Consequently, the Australians withdrew a short distance and consolidated their positions. In XIII Corps, 151st Brigade pushed north-eastwards but suffered heavy casualties from 21. Reserve-Division positions east of Gouy. The brigade was able to secure Gouy and Le Catelet by 1030hrs, and 149th Brigade partially closed the gap between these villages and Vendhuille by 1130hrs.

Having cleared the Hindenburg Reserve Line in their initial attack, 139th and 137th Brigades soon pushed on towards Montbrehain. 139th Brigade used hedgerows and sunken lanes to infiltrate troops through heavy machine-gun fire that was sweeping across their front from the high ground to the north. Their last remaining tank cleared a large nest of German machine guns in front of the village, and following a sharp fight amongst the streets and houses, Montbrehain was secured around 1130hrs. On the right, 137th Brigade was continuing its hard slog. Not only was their front extended as they advanced further east, but the ongoing fight between 32nd Division and 221. Infanterie-Division in Sequehart also required them to deploy a flank guard. The diminishing numbers of infantry were able to establish a foothold at the base of Mannequin Hill, south of Montbrehain, but they could not force the troops of 34. Infanterie-Division from its crest.

Having breached the Hindenburg Reserve Line, word was sent to 5th Cavalry Brigade to begin its move forwards to begin the exploitation phase of the operation. However, cavalry patrols, supported by Whippet tanks, sent forwards from Montbrehain, reported stiffening opposition, and the brigade commander called off the action and withdrew his troops into the reserve of 46th Division.

I Bayerische-Armeekorps and 51. Generalkommando were not slow to recognize the crisis now unfolding on the boundary between them. The situation at Montbrehain was made the priority, and in the late morning, the exhausted troops of 2. Garde-Division were recalled to block the Roman road against any Australian advance from the north. They were backed up by 20. Infanterie-Division, which was recalled from Caudry to Prémont. Both divisions had assumed they would be heading for a rest period after enduring prolonged combat over the preceding days. At the same time, the leading battalions of 24. Infanterie-Division were formed into a composite regiment and assembled, ready to counter-attack Montbrehain from the north, while Infanterie-Regiment 30 of 34. Infanterie-Division was directed to do likewise from the south. Concurrently, Infanterie-Regiment 145, from 34. Infanterie-Division, was ordered to retake Sequehart.

The first counter-attack was launched at 1230hrs by Infanterie-Regiment 30. The British protective barrage fell behind the German assault troops, who advanced under rifle and machine-gun fire from British troops in Ramicourt. This failed to stop them, and they had soon occupied a threatening position to the south-west of 139th Brigade in Montbrehain. As this situation developed to his rear right, the commander, Brig. Harington, observed the assault of 24. Infanterie-Division approaching from the north-east. Facing the prospect of being surrounded, he quickly ordered the withdrawal from the village to a line east of Ramicourt. There, his troops formed a position in the sunken roads running north to south and held off any further German attempt to advance towards them.

In the evening, Endres' troops launched their final attempts to regain their lost positions. At 1900hrs, 221. and 34. Infanterie-Divisions attacked down the western slope of Mannequin Hill, driving back 137th Brigade. However, in a see-saw action over the next three hours, British counter-attacks and artillery fire drove the Germans back across the summit which became no man's land for the coming night. At 1930hrs, 221. Infanterie-Division also attacked Sequehart behind a strong barrage, but the troops of 14th and 97th Brigades had spent the day developing their defensive positions and fought off the German infantry with rifle and machine-gun fire alone.

In the French sector, de Fonclare's 15e Corps continued its attempts to cross the river Somme and the Somme Canal but was unable to push the left flank of I Bayerische Armeekorps from its positions. In the late afternoon 126e Division relieved the

Mannequin Hill from the south-west. Montbrehain is on the skyline. 30. Infanterie-Division held the crest of the hill from 46th Division between 3 and 5 October 1918. (Author)

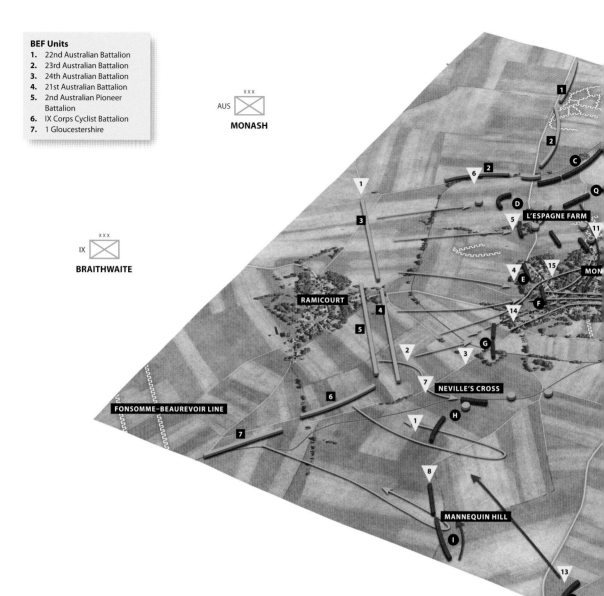

BEF Units

1. 22nd Australian Battalion
2. 23rd Australian Battalion
3. 24th Australian Battalion
4. 21st Australian Battalion
5. 2nd Australian Pioneer Battalion
6. IX Corps Cyclist Battalion
7. 1 Gloucestershire

AUS ⊠ ××× MONASH

IX ⊠ ××× BRAITHWAITE

MONASH

L'ESPAGNE FARM

RAMICOURT

FONSOMME–BEAUREVOIR LINE

NEVILLE'S CROSS

MANNEQUIN HILL

EVENTS

1. 0605hrs: barrage opens from eight brigades of Australian field artillery. Barrage advances 100yds every four minutes. 21st and 24th Australian Battalions advance.

2. Barrage falls short on the right and hits 21st Australian Battalion.

3. The foremost positions of III/30 engage Capt. Sullivan's company in 21st Battalion with machine-gun fire from quarries and houses on south-western edge of village. These were cleared by Australians, during which time, Capt. Sullivan is killed and company taken over by Lt. McConnachie.

4. In 21st Battalion, Capt. Hoad's and Capt. Mahoney's companies clear I/133 and I/139 from the western edge of the village.

5. In 24th Battlion, Capt. Pollington's company clears II/474 and remnants of IR 472 from l'Espagne Farm strongpoint. Lieutenant Ingram wins the VC, capturing 63 Germans with 40 machine guns.

6. In 24th Battalion, Capt. Fletcher's company held up by fire from village and high ground which killed and wounded all officers.

7. 2nd Australian Pioneers held up by machine-gun fire from the right flank. Lieutenant Wilkinson works two Australian machine guns on to the German left flank to clear the position, killing 30, wounding 50 and capturing 14 machine guns.

8. IX Corps Cyclist Battalion and 1 Gloucestershire clear I/30 from the north-western part of Mannequin Hill. Further advance halted by machine-gun fire from Doon Mill, and IR 67 from east and south.

9. Capt. McConnachie's company clears the main street with tanks from 16th Tank Battalion and advance south towards Doon Mill. Fire from II/474 and FAR 48 in Doon Mill stops the Australians. Their return fire halts a II/474 counter-attack. McConnachie's company and 2nd Australian Pioneers set up posts to secure southern perimeter of village.

10. Capt. Hoad's company clears the eastern part of village and sets up posts facing Brancourt.

11. Capt. Mahoney's company clears the north-eastern part of the village and a cemetery to the north and establishes perimeter posts.

12. 0830hrs: counter-attack by 9/67 and I/67 drives 1 Gloucestershire and IX Corps Cyclist Battalion back to original positions, less posts maintained with 2nd Australian Pioneer Battalion around Neville's Cross.

13. 0900hrs: I/179 launches a counter-attack from the north-west. I and II/77 launch counter-attack from north and north-east. II and III/139, with II/179, counter-attack from Brancourt.

14. 1000hrs: Capt. Mahoney withdraws posts to south-western edge of village when short of ammunition. I and II/77 advance to church in centre of village. Capt. McConnachie holds his positions and fights off attacks from the east.

15. 1015hrs: two platoons from Capt. Hardwick's company in reserve are ordered to outflank the Germans in the village from the north. I/179, I and II/77 subsequently withdraw. Australian posts re-established on perimeter of village and Montbrehain secured.

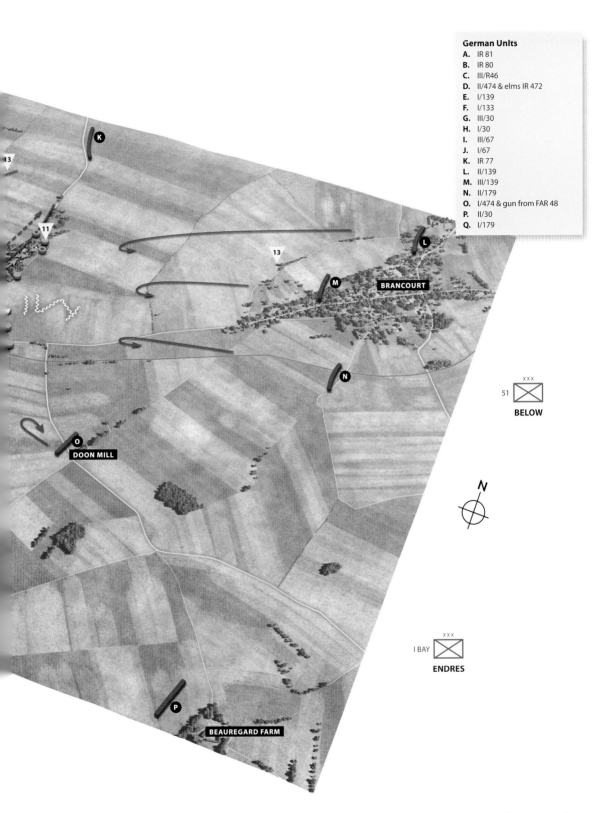

German Units

A. IR 81
B. IR 80
C. III/R46
D. II/474 & elms IR 472
E. I/139
F. I/133
G. III/30
H. I/30
I. III/67
J. I/67
K. IR 77
L. II/139
M. III/139
N. II/179
O. I/474 & gun from FAR 48
P. II/30
Q. I/179

K

13

11

13

L

M

BRANCOURT

N

51 ⊠ BELOW

O

DOON MILL

I BAY ⊠ ENDRES

P

BEAUREGARD FARM

N

THE LAST RIDGE
2nd Australian Division's capture of Montbrehain

British 1st Division south of Sequehart and prepared to advance towards Fontaine-Uterte and Frensoy-le-Grand. At 1730hrs, 36e and 31e Corps made limited gains at Harly. 8e Corps attacked the Hindenburg Line defences at Alaincourt at 1530hrs with little effect, as Watter's XXVI Reservekorps held them in the Outpost Line with a combination of artillery and infantry fire.

Late in the evening, Rawlinson issued his orders for the following day. IX Corps was to secure Mannequin Hill, while the Australian Corps was to clear the high ground north-west of Montbrehain. XIII Corps was to secure Beaurevoir and Prospect Hill. In order to relieve the tiring troops of IX Corps, 2nd Australian Division was to slip to the right and in turn be relieved on the left by XIII Corps' 25th Division, which was moving up from the rear. Coordination of this manoeuvre was made more complicated as the position of many of the front-line battalions was uncertain following the German counter-attacks in the afternoon and evening.

A NOTE IS PREPARED, 4 OCTOBER

Withdrawal from the canal – the battle of the Beaurevoir Line
The overnight insertion of 25th Division did not go smoothly. After a 20km approach march, the British 7th Brigade relieved the 7th Australian Brigade between 0100hrs and 0200hrs. Fatigued and disorientated, the British brigade and battalion staffs attempted to complete their preparations for the coming attack in poor visibility, unclear as to the exact locations of their units.

Under a blanket of thick fog, at 0600hrs the leading troops of 6th Australian Brigade attacked behind a heavy artillery barrage and by 0830hrs had secured the ridge between Montbrehain and Beaurevoir. On their left, however, the efforts of 7th Brigade to envelop Beaurevoir were undermined by the overnight confusion. Orders for the left-hand battalion were received too late to advance on time. Separated from the supporting barrage, the infantry was soon brought to a halt by heavy machine-gun fire from 119. Infanterie-Division overlooking them from the village. The right-hand attack had more luck and fought its way into Beaurevoir from the south. However, it was soon counter-attacked, and by 1310hrs it had withdrawn to the south-west where it consolidated its line with the Australians.

On the left of Fourth Army, 50th Division also attacked at 0600hrs. Six battalions of 149th and 150th Brigades, supported by 11 brigades of artillery, attacked 21. Reserve- and 54. Infanterie-Divisions' positions at Le Catelet and Gouy. Despite being stalled by a resolute defence, a renewed effort by the British reserve units outflanked Le Catelet from the north and secured the junction with Third Army on their left.

Across the bare slopes of Mannequin Hill, IX Corps and I Bayerische Armeekorps slugged away at each other to little effect. The exhausted troops of 46th Division were reinforced by the Corps Cyclist Battalion, the dismounted troops of 5th Cavalry Brigade, 2nd Life Guards Machine Gun Battalion and 3rd Brigade. The commander and chief of staff of the latter were killed by shellfire while reconnoitring their new positions. In turn, the British

Beaurevoir from the west. The overgrown railway embankment on the forward edge of the village formed the firing line for 119. Infanterie-Division. Machine-gun and trench mortar fire swept the fields in the foreground as 25th Division attacked on 5 October 1918. (Author)

The battles of the Beaurevoir Line and Cambrai 1918

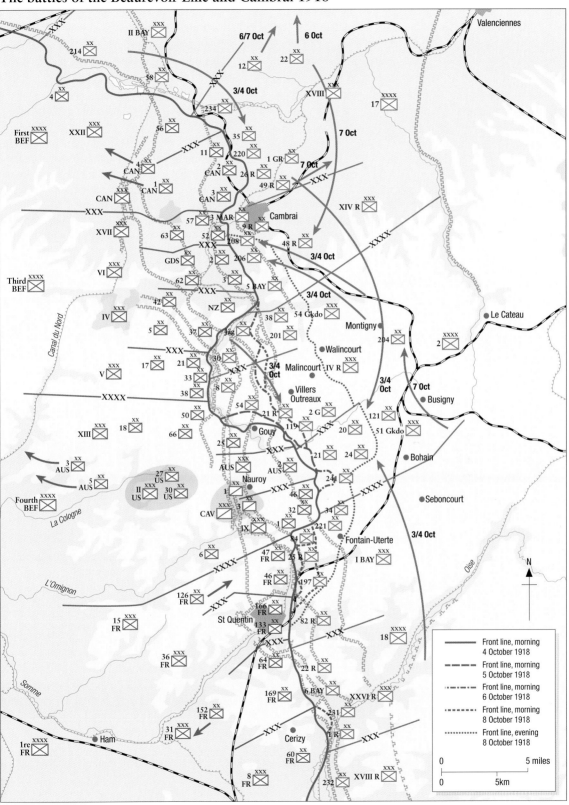

Legend:

————	Front line, morning 4 October 1918
– – –	Front line, morning 5 October 1918
–·–·–	Front line, morning 6 October 1918
·······	Front line, morning 8 October 1918
·········	Front line, evening 8 October 1918

0 — 5 miles

0 — 5km

N

German troops launch an attack through a burning village. (IWM, Q88075)

artillery fire raked across the exposed troops of Infanterie-Regiment 30 at the top of the hill throughout the day. In these trying conditions, the infantry from both sides consolidated their positions and prepared for the following days as best they could.

The French 1re Armée also attacked in the early morning, with 15e Corps attempting to force a crossing of the Somme at Morcourt at 0630hrs. Two battalions of 46e Division drove elements of 197. Infanterie-Division out of the village and hung on to their bridgehead despite several counter-attacks during the day. At 1030hrs, 47e Division attempted to push forwards between Sequehart and Lesdins but could make only limited gains against a determined defence by 221. and 84. Infanterie-Divisions. Further south, 36e Corps had an equally difficult day as machine-gun and artillery fire stalled their efforts to push through the industrial suburbs south-east of St Quentin. On their right, 31e Corps was pushed back across the main St Quentin–La Fere road by a German attack during the morning, but was able to regain its original positions, with a counter-attack at 1330hrs at a cost in the day of 15 killed and 43 wounded. Meanwhile, at 1730 hrs, 8e Corps was able to seize Hill 116 west of Berthenicourt at a cost of 32 casualties.

The limited gains made by Debeney's men had their inevitable consequence at 1000hrs. Frustrated by the lack of progress and pestered by repeated complaints by Haig over his dissatisfaction with 1re Armée, Foch reached down past Pétain at GQG, to deliver a pointed personal telephone message to Fayolle at GAR, reinforcing the necessity for 1re Armée to improve its performance. He then made the stinging observation to Pétain that the French Army's performance lacked effective command and drive, a somewhat harsh rebuke given the demands on Pétain's army to support three of the four major Allied attacks and the difficult terrain of the Meuse-Argonne region.

In the British Fourth Army, Rawlinson continued to drive his men forwards after a disappointing day. At 1830hrs he issued orders directing the Australian Corps to secure Montbrehain, while IX Corps seized Mannequin and Doon Hills. XIII Corps was to secure Beaurevoir in conjunction with 38th Division of Third Army. However, perhaps in recognition of the tenacious German defence, the Cavalry Corps was stood down from one hour's notice to four hours' notice to move.

While Rawlinson was attenuating his expectations, Haig had no such doubts. At 1900hrs he outlined his intent to exploit the success gained by his forces by following up 2. Armee and 17. Armee before they could re-establish a new defensive position. He directed his staff to draft orders for a major attack by Third and Fourth Armies supported by mounted troops to reach the line of Bohain–Busigny–Le Cateau–Solesmes. First Army was to cross the Schelde Canal and the Schelde at Ramillies to protect the left flank of Third Army. The French 1re Armée's advance towards Fontaine-Uterte and Croix Fonsomme was to protect the right of Fourth Army.

Although Fourth Army had not achieved the breakthrough Rawlinson sought, its efforts to widen the breach did have a positive effect. The seizure of the high ground around Le Catelet now threatened the left flank of IV

Reservekorps and 54. Generalkommando. As a result, orders were issued to evacuate the Hindenburg Support Line and withdraw back to the Hindenburg Reserve Line between Crèvecoeur and Beaurevoir. Byng's Third Army would no longer be required to fight its way over the Schelde Canal.

Meanwhile, overnight in Berlin, the Germans finally despatched their note to President Wilson requesting a cessation of hostilities and the commencement of negotiations based on the Fourteen Point programme Wilson articulated to Congress in January.

THE LAST 'COOEE', 5 OCTOBER

Victory at Montbrehain – the battle of the Beaurevoir Line

While the German note made its way to Washington, Rawlinson's troops assembled for their next strike. The attack on Montbrehain was to be launched by the last remaining fresh troops of Rosenthal's 2nd Australian Division: the 21st and 24th Infantry and 2nd Pioneer Battalions. While the Pioneers relieved 139th Brigade in front of Montbrehain at midnight, the troops of the 21st and 24th Battalions moved into their assault positions through a heavy German bombardment of the Australian battery positions behind Ramicourt. This shelling delayed the 12 tanks that were due to support them. Facing them were the battered remnants of 241. Infanterie-Division reinforced by 24. Infanterie-Division. At 0605hrs the barrage from eight brigades of field artillery struck the German lines, although some of the rounds fell amongst the Australians on the right. Despite this setback, the Australian infantry soon fought their way through into the village where the tanks arrived to support them. Posts were set up around the northern, eastern and southern perimeters from where, around 0900hrs, the Australian sentries detected the gradual assembly of German infantry groups in preparation for a counter-attack. By 1000hrs the reserve battalions of 24. Infanterie-Division had driven the Australian line back to the western edge of Montbrehain. Two Australian reserve platoons then swung around the western and northern sides of the village before striking the right flank of the German assault. By midday, the Australians had re-established possession of Montbrehain, from which they repelled several further German counter-attacks during the afternoon. By 1700hrs the fighting died down and in the night the Australians were relieved by 118th Regiment of 30th (US) Division. The action proved to be the last battle fought by the Australian infantry in the European theatre in World War 1.

Unfortunately, IX Corps' attempts to support the Australian effort proved unsuccessful against the heavy defensive fire sweeping the open slopes of Doon and Mannequin Hills. Although 3rd Brigade established posts on the latter, they were driven back to their starting positions by the afternoon counter-attacks.

To the north, XIII Corps finally secured Beaurevoir despite the determined efforts of 119. Infanterie-Division to hold their position. Lieutenant-General Morland's plan directed 25th Division to attack after an 80-minute bombardment from the corps' heavy artillery.

Montbrehain and L'Espagne Farm from the north. The farm and the quarry just visible to the right formed a strongpoint for Infanterie-Regiments 472 and 474. Captain G. M. Ingram MM of the 24th Australian Infantry Battalion won the Victoria Cross here, capturing over 90 prisoners and 40 machine guns from dugouts and cellars on 5 October 1918. (IWM, E(AUS) 3775)

The buildings on the outskirts of the village bristled with machine guns, which held off the infantry of 7th and 74th Brigades, despite their supporting tanks briefly penetrating the German positions. Anti-tank rifles drove these off and the attack stalled until the afternoon. At 1840hrs, 7th and 75th Brigades assaulted once more after a further heavy artillery bombardment and this time they succeeded in clearing the village, having caught the defenders by surprise. The attacks continued overnight and by 0500hrs the high ground to the north and south were in British hands.

On the left of XIII Corps, 50th Division quickly discovered the deserted positions east of Vendhuille and cooperated with 38th Division in V Corps to advance the army boundary to Aubencheul-aux-Bois. This coincided with similar activity across Third Army, as the morning patrols reported the absence of German troops in the canal defences. V Corps troops used whatever materials were at hand to improvise the means to cross the canal and by 1500hrs had occupied the Hindenburg Support Line 2,000m further east. To the north, IV Corps noticed the German artillery shelling the recently evacuated positions and soon organized its units to follow up. The front line was quickly re-established against the Germans in the Hindenburg Reserve Line, and by 1800hrs, engineers had opened bridges for wheeled traffic to cross the canal.

In the French sector, 15e Corps continued their efforts to break the left flank of I Bayerische Armeekorps. At 1000hrs, 46e Division drove the exhausted troops of 84. Infanterie-Division out of Lesdins only to be swept back to the western edge of the village by a counter-attack in the middle of the day. They were not to be denied their goal, however, and another French effort at 1800hrs seized the village once and for all. South of St Quentin, 31e Corps made limited progress towards Neuville-St-Amand, with 64e Division's attack at 1430hrs being repulsed by machine-gun fire and grenades. To the south, 8e Corps limited its activity to patrols, capturing nine prisoners from 237. Infanterie-Division at Servais.

The directive issued by Haig to his staff the previous night was briefed to Rawlinson, Horne and Byng at a conference hosted by Fourth Army's HQ. Haig's Chief of Staff outlined the proposed scheme for Fourth Army to seize the line Wassigny–Le Cateau–Valenciennes as rapidly as possible, with the Cavalry Corps in close support. Third and First Armies were to cooperate to secure the left flank, with a simultaneous attack if possible. The operation was scheduled to commence on 7 October, but it was postponed for 24 hours following delays in bringing forward artillery ammunition.

PREPARING THE LAST BLOW, 6–7 OCTOBER

Over the next two days, Rawlinson and Byng's armies prepared themselves for the coming attack. The artillery began to fire the counter-battery programme immediately and engaged other key points in the German defences. Meanwhile, supporting barrages were planned to protect the attacking troops as they moved forward. Minor operations were undertaken by II (US) Corps, XIII Corps and V Corps to improve their assault positions, although the latter was ejected from its gains in Villers Outreaux. In II (US) Corps, Maj. Gen. Read successfully appealed to Pershing to return the officers from their AEF training schools as he rehabilitated his units from their recent battle casualties.

North of St Quentin, Gen. de Fonclare's 15e Corps continued its attempt to turn the Hindenburg Line facing the rest of 1re Armée. At 1400hrs, the French assaulted either side of Remaucourt in an attempt to work around the right flank of Hutier's 18. Armee, with 46e Division securing the high ground to the south, while 47e Division did likewise to the north. 46e Division then fought its way through to the eastern edge of the village, although a counter-attack by 197. Infanterie-Division drove the French back to the centre, where the French consolidated their line. Having advanced 1.5–2km at a cost of 555 casualties, de Fonclare's men were becoming more aggressive, and their attacks now posed a direct threat to the lines of communication for the German troops to the south. The French assault resumed at 1500hrs the following day, with 46e Division attacking the Tilloy Farm on the ridge south of Remaucourt. After a hard fight, the position was secured and shortly after the French troops followed up by driving the remaining Germans out of Remaucourt itself. To the north, however, 47e Division was unable to dislodge the defenders in Bellecourt Farm, where heavy machine-gun and artillery fire prevented any significant advance to the east. 36e Corps covered the southern flank of these operations by securing the ridge between Remaucourt and Rouvroy.

In an effort to shore up what remained of the crumbling Hindenburg Line defences, the Germans continued to shuffle their worn-out units along the battlefront and replace those that they could with fresher units from quieter sectors. On 6 October, Rupprecht withdrew 22. Infanterie-Division and sent it to II Bayerische Armeekorps, where it relieved 48. Reserve-Division at Douai. In turn, 48. Reserve-Division was then redeployed to XIV Reservekorps, where it relieved 3. Marine-Division at Niergnes. Meanwhile, having spent two days travelling from Lorraine, 204. Infanterie-Division detrained at Bertry and deployed to Prémont with IV Reservekorps. Only now were the desperately needed reserves from east of the Meuse belatedly reaching the battlefront on the Hindenburg Line. They were too few in number and they were too late.

ENDGAME, 8 OCTOBER

Clearing the last line – the battle of Cambrai, 1918

As the rain fell through the early hours of the morning, the Allied assault troops made their way to the jumping-off lines while the gunners continued to pound their German counterparts. The attack was to commence on the front of Third Army, where Byng's troops attempted to bring themselves level with

Fourth Army as a preliminary to their combined assault at 0510hrs. Byng's four corps were to secure the line from Walincourt to Niergnes, and so doing, seize the last vestige of the Hindenburg Reserve Line remaining in German hands, between Lesdain and Villers Outreaux. In this manner, it was hoped to force the Germans to relinquish Cambrai by threatening its envelopment from north and south. Fourth Army was to drive along the Roman Road towards Le Cateau, with an objective set 6km ahead along the Cambrai–Bohain road. With Boehn's troops now deprived of any constructed field defences, Kavanagh's Cavalry Corps were to be ready to strike forwards if the German units broke. Debeney's 1re Armée was to cover Rawlinson's right and widen the breach towards Fresnoy-le-Grand and Seboncourt if possible. Horne's Canadian Corps was to cooperate with artillery support and infantry demonstrations to deceive the German forces north of Cambrai and hold them in position.

On the German side, Hutier, Carlowitz and Below were to continue to delay the Allies as long as possible in order to buy time for the construction of the Hermann Position to continue behind them. As a belated addition to the forces available to the German troops around Cambrai, XIV Reservekorps had secured the use of some German tank units, equipped with captured British Mk. IV tanks, and assigned them to the divisions guarding the southern flank of the town.

Byng's preliminary assault got underway at 0100hrs in V Corps, with 38th Division's attack at Villers Outreaux. From the outset, however, strong wire defences of the Reserve Hindenburg Line, covered by the alert and aggressive troops of GenMaj. Hamman's 8. Infanterie-Division, brought the advance to a complete halt in the darkness. Only after daybreak, when the artillery barrage was brought back onto the village and a handful of tanks flattened paths through the wire, could the Welshmen storm the trenches and buildings behind. This task was not complete until mid-morning, and the coordinated attack that was due to move forwards with Fourth Army's advance from its first objective at 0800hrs was postponed until 1130hrs. On the left of V Corps, by contrast, 21st Division had little difficulty in driving the inner flanks of 8. and 30. Infanterie-Divisions out of the Reserve Hindenburg Line in its sector. Not realizing that the right of V Corps' advance had stalled, 62nd Brigade commenced the advance to the second objective at 0800hrs as planned, but was harassed by fire from the front and from Villers Outreaux on the right flank. However, slow but steady progress was made until 1800hrs, when the advance halted west of Walincourt. 38th Division's delayed attack finally got underway at 1150hrs. Malincourt was enveloped and the battered remains of 8. Infanterie-Division retired under the cover of fire from a nearby gun battery to the high ground west of Elincourt, where the British advance halted for the day.

In Harper's IV Corps, 37th and the New Zealand Divisions were tasked with clearing the Hindenburg Reserve Line south of Lesdain before advancing to the final objective at Esnes. The attack was launched at 0430hrs, with 37th Division's 111th Brigade driving Jägerregiment 11 out of the Bel Aise salient before swinging south to clear the remainder of the trench lines from the right flank. This done, 112th Brigade arrived to take over the advance, but after a 7km approach march overnight, it was engaged by German positions that had been overlooked in the dark. This separated them from the supporting barrage, but, undeterred, they fought forwards using classic infantry 'fire and movement', until at 1020hrs, the division objective was secured. In the New Zealand Division's sector, 2nd and 3rd New Zealand Brigades punched through the wire and trenches west of Lesdains before enveloping the village from north and south. Having cleared the buildings of 38. Infanterie-Division's surviving troops, the Kiwis continued their advance despite coming under fire from Séranvillers and Esnes. They secured the latter village by mid-morning and shattered Infanterie-Regiment 94 in the process. The German unit subsequently reported 90 per cent of its men as lost in the battle.

Bel Aise Farm from the south-west. The farm was a strongpoint in the Hindenburg Reserve Line which climbed out of the valley and ran north–south through the farm complex. The white buildings in the valley to the left of the farm are in Lesdain. Haig visited this spot on 9 October 1918. (Author)

The attack of Haldane's VI Corps was complicated by the need to give space for 63rd Division, in XVII Corps, to assault Niergnes from the south-west. This resulted in VI Corps' sector widening from 2,000m to 3,000m as the advance moved eastwards. The attack of 2nd and 3rd Divisions went well at first, with 9th and 99th Brigades quickly clearing the trenches west of Séranvillers. However, as they moved forwards to the second objective on the Cambrai–Bohain road, the widening front exposed them to heavy machine-gun fire which caused significant casualties. Although this was unable to deny them their objective apart from around La Targette, they were in a weakened and vulnerable position. Fergusson's XVII Corps had recalled the veteran 63rd Division back into the line to lead its attack before it was sent for a well-earned rest. Nine brigades of field artillery and four brigades of heavy artillery blasted two battalions of 188th and 189th Brigades through the first objective, which was seized shortly after 0600hrs. The Royal Marines and the Hood Battalion had a much tougher fight, with Reserve-Ersatz-Infanterie-Regiment 4 on the southern edge of Niergnes, but by 0800hrs had secured the village and took up position on its eastern edge.

At this point Morgen launched a desperate counter-attack with infantry supported by tanks and heavy artillery fire, in an attempt to drive the British back. At 0830, troops from 5. Bayerische-Infanterie-Division, supported by two tanks of Tank-Abteilung 16, struck the New Zealanders from the direction of Wambaix. However, the German vehicles were destroyed by British tanks from 12th Tank Battalion, who diverted from their allotted mission in support of 3rd Division to the north, and Esnes was held. Further north, elements of 48th Reserve Division supported by five tanks attacked the weakened units of 2nd and 3rd Divisions at Séranvillers and drove them back to the western edge of the village before two German tanks were destroyed and the line held. Reserve-Infanterie-Regiment 65, supported by four vehicles of Tank-Abteilung 15, attacked the Royal Marines and Hood Battalion at Niergnes from Awoingt. Assuming that the familiar shapes approaching them were friendly, the British allowed them to get within 50m before the Germans opened fire and disabused them of their error. The British tanks present were quickly disabled and the infantry fell back through the village. However, the British soon regained their composure, and fought back with a captured German field gun and an anti-tank rifle. Two of the German tanks were destroyed and the other two withdrew, leaving the Hood Battalion to retake the village after an artillery bombardment.

In the confused situation across the front of Third Army, brigade commanders struggled to coordinate their counter-moves effectively, with attacks at 1300hrs and 1500hrs being hacked apart by German machine-

TANK ABTEILUNG: GERMAN COUNTER-ATTACK AT NIERGNES, 8 OCTOBER 1918 (PP. 84–85)

Although the German Army made limited attempts to develop armoured vehicles from 1914 onwards, it was the appearance of the first British tanks on the Somme in 1916 that galvanized their efforts. However, competing design proposals bedevilled developments in 1917, with only 20 A7V vehicles produced by the end of the war. These were supplemented, however, by the re-commissioning of British tanks captured on the Western Front from the battle of Cambrai in November 1917 onwards. The gun-armed 'male' vehicles were re-armed with the Maxim-Nordfeldt 57mm gun, while the machine-gun-armed 'female' vehicles had their Lewis guns adapted to fire German-calibre ammunition. These vehicles were also armed with the Mauser 12.7mm anti-tank rifle to give them some protection against British 'male' tanks if they were encountered. These captured vehicles, or *Beutepanzers*, were organized in six units, each consisting of two 'male' and three 'female' tanks. By September 1918 the A7Vs equipped schwere Kampfwagen Abteilungen 1 and 2, with the captured vehicles equipping schwere Kampfwagen Abteilungen 11–16. In their preparations for the battle on the Hindenburg Line, OHL initially deployed these units behind Heeresgruppe Kronprinz, but in early October, Abteilungen 1, 11, 13, 15 and 16 were redeployed to Cambrai to meet the British threat. On the morning of 8 October, Abteilungen 15 and 16 were assembled in Awoingt in support of XIV Reservekorps.

Soon after daybreak, Third Army's VI and XVII Corps were consolidating their positions south of Cambrai. The 188th and 189th Brigades of 63rd Division were tasked with securing XVII Corps' second objective east of Niergnes along the Cambrai–Esnes road in conjunction with the Mk. IV tanks L6, L9, L12 and

L16 of A Company, 12th Tank Battalion around 0800hrs **(1)**. At this point Morgen's XIV Reservekorps ordered a counter-attack and at 0830hrs commander of RIR 221, Maj. Gluszewski, led his reserve unit, II/RIR 221, and four tanks of schwere Kampfwagen Abteilung 15 under the command of Oberlt Knoop **(2)**, along the shallow valley from Awoingt to counter-attack Niergnes. The British protective barrage caused some disruption to the German troops, but the smoke and dust also reduced visibility for the British as they reorganized their new line. The familiar silhouettes approaching from the east did not cause any immediate alarm, as it was assumed that they were vehicles from flanking units that were returning from a deeper penetration of the German lines. The leading German tanks got within 50m when they opened fire **(3)**. The gun-armed tanks 218 and 219 quickly knocked out L16 with two simultaneous hits from their 57mm weapons, while 12.7mm rounds disabled L6, L9 and L12. The British infantry began to withdraw back through Niergnes as a confused mêlée broke out on the slopes east of the village. In a somewhat ironic turn of events, the commanding officers of the 63rd (Royal Naval) Division's Anson and Hood Battalions, alongside the members of the disembarked tank crews, brought an abandoned German field gun and some Mauser anti-tank rifles back into action against their former owners. *Beutepanzer* 219 was destroyed by this gunfire and their remaining three withdrew. For the rest of the morning II/RIR221 was heavily attacked by 188th and 189th Brigades and suffered heavy casualties including the commanding officer, Haupt. Kohlrausch, and his three company commanders. Major Gluszewski and his staff were captured, and as their strength declined, the remaining Germans were driven back to Awoingt.

gun fire. Furthermore, 63rd Division was pushed back another 300m following another German attack, this time supported by one tank. Only in late afternoon was Haldane able to re-impose some order, with 2nd and 3rd Divisions directed to launch a coordinated attack under a strong artillery barrage at 1800hrs, which drove the Germans back over the Cambrai–Esnes road. This re-established British control over the battlefield, although the forward troops were withdrawn slightly overnight to enable the road to mark to barrage line for the following day.

The Mauser Tankgewehr M-1918. This weapon was brought into service in May 1918. It fired a 13.2mm armour-piercing round with a muzzle velocity of 785m/s, and could penetrate 22mm of armour at 100m range. The T-Gewehr weighed 15.9kg and 15,800 were manufactured. (IWM, Q11264)

On the left flank of Fourth Army, XIII Corps had to contend with a defence that was now thoroughly alert following Third Army's unsuccessful overnight efforts to secure Villers Outreaux. The assault troops assembled under heavy machine-gun and artillery fire and intermittent attacks by German night bombers. However, some troops of Conta's IV Reservekorps were showing clear signs of fatigue, having been in line continuously since the battle opened 12 days earlier. Moving off on the right at 0520hrs, 25th Division had little trouble pushing back 121. Infanterie-Division and by 0720hrs was on the first objective with 300 prisoners in the bag. On the left, however, although 66th Division had reached the same line, they had a much tougher time from enfilade fire from 8. Infanterie-Division in Villers Outreaux. Notwithstanding this minor setback, Morland's troops commenced their advance to the second objective on time at 0810hrs, reaching the villages of Élincourt and Serain by 1900hrs.

On the right flank IX Corps' infantry also attacked at 0520hrs, finally driving the Germans from their positions on Mannequin and Doon Hills. On the right, however, the assault broke down as 1re Armée was not due to attack until 0600hrs. Fire from unsuppressed German positions in the French sector quickly disabled the British tanks supporting 6th Division advancing to the north. When Debeney's 15e Corps did attack, 47e Division hammered away at Bellecourt Farm, while its flanking units enveloped the position to the north and south. Unable to supress the German machine-gun positions at the farm, however, the attack stalled. Meanwhile, uncoordinated attacks by the British 6th Division failed to make any headway, until a combined assault was organized with the French around 1300hrs. This unlocked the stalemate on the British front north of Fontaine-Uterte and opened the way for the French infantry to finally encircle Bellecourt Farm, capturing 500 German troops from 11 different regiments in the process. Having cleared

Infantry of 30th (US) Division attacking Prémont on 8 October 1918. (IWM, Q7084)

this bastion in the German lines, both the British and the French began to push back the right flank of I Bayerische Armeekorps as it withdrew to Fresnoy. By 2200hrs the British had secured the ridge running north from Méricourt, while the French moved into Fontaine-Uterte and Essigny-le-Petit. To the south of 15e Corps, 36e Corps secured Rouvroy and the high ground to the north-east.

In the centre of Fourth Army, 30th (US) Division led II (US) Corps' assault, with 118th and 117th Infantry Regiments ordered to advance 6km and

9th Lancers returning from Prémont on 8 October 1918. Kavanagh's corps never quite got the opportunity to repeat its achievements at Amiens. However, units and sub-units of mounted troops remained an integral part of the 'all-arms' advanced guards that the BEF formed to maintain contact with the retreating Germans. (IWM, Q80447)

secure the villages of Brancourt and Prémont. The infantry was to be supported by 20 Mk. V tanks of the American 301st Tank Battalion and 16 Whippets of the British 6th Tank Battalion. In contrast to their earlier battle at Bony, this time the American infantry had the benefit of a solid artillery barrage to crush the defences as they approached. The positions in open country were quickly mopped up, and by 0800hrs, the leading troops were on their first objective. However, the large number of machine guns in Brancourt brought progress to a halt, and it was 1100hrs before a combined assault with 301st Tank Battalion cleared the village. The advance then pushed on towards Prémont, where again German rearguards from the exhausted men from 20. Infanterie-Division, reinforced by Infanterie-Regiment 25, held them up with machine-gun fire. This time the Whippet tanks of 6th Tank Battalion moved forwards to assist, and by mid-afternoon the Americans had seized the village and began to dig in. In securing their objectives for the day, 30th (US) Division had captured 1,500 prisoners and earned three Medals of Honor in the process: they were rapidly improving their combat skills on the Western Front.

Following up the attacks by IX, II (US) and XIII Corps was Kavanagh's Cavalry Corps. By 0700hrs, 1st and 3rd Cavalry Divisions were west of Nauroy and south of Joncourt respectively. At 0950hrs, the leading regiments of 1st Cavalry Division pressed forwards between Prémont and Serain but were halted by machine-gun fire to their front. Further south some cavalry troops managed to attack German artillery batteries with swords drawn, but by 1440hrs Kavanagh reported that the German rearguards could only be cleared with excessive losses. In the knowledge that Haig wanted to keep his mounted force intact, at 1630hrs he ordered his troops back to the relative safety of their early morning assembly areas.

As the weather cleared in the morning, the aircraft of V Brigade RAF played an increasingly important role in the action. While contact aircraft fed a constant stream of information on the progress of the battle to the RAF's Central Information Bureau, 35 Squadron dropped smoke bombs to shroud the advance of XIII Corps from the high ground around Serain and maintained the smokescreen by relays of aircraft between 0600hrs and

Canadian troops moving into the burning remains of Cambrai. (IWM, CO3373)

0800hrs. When German columns were seen around Clary in the afternoon, 208 Squadron – held for just such a task – was despatched to disperse the increasingly harassed German troops.

As the fighting died down at dusk, the formidable fortifications of the Hindenburg Line finally lay behind the Allied armies. Although German troops were still in Cambrai, the town was now threatened with envelopment from north and south and its retention was no longer tenable. Orders were given late in the day for the overnight withdrawal to the Hermann Stellung along the line of the river Selle 15km to the east. While the battle of Cambrai 1918 would last officially until 12 October, the battle for the Hindenburg Line in its meaningful sense was over.

AFTERMATH

The consequences of the battle were as profound as any on the Western Front during the entire war. It not only shaped the final actions on the battlefield, but it also fundamentally set the timetable for peace and crafted the terms on which the Armistice was signed.

Defeat on the Hindenburg Line meant that OHL had nowhere near enough time to prepare the Hermann Stellung to the degree necessary to repel the BEF. Retiring under heavy attack from the RAF, the Germans hurriedly took up position behind the river Selle, where the British advance guards closed up to them on 13 October. Having taken four days to bring forward artillery and logistic support, Rawlinson's Fourth Army launched its attack at 0520hrs on 17 October with XIII, II (US) and IX Corps driving over the

The commander of 137th Brigade, Brig. J. V. Campbell VC addressing his men at Riqueval Bridge on 2 October 1918. Several of the men are wearing the life jackets taken from the cross-Channel steamers and used in the assault over the canal. (IWM, Q9534)

river between Le Cateau and the Forest of Andigny. Although resistance was unexpectedly heavy, IX Corps advanced 4.5km, with Fourth and French 1re Armies taking 5,200 prisoners. The attack was resumed at 0530hrs the next day, and by the end of 19 October, Rawlinson's and Debeney's men had torn a hole in the Hermann Stellung 11km wide and 9km deep. Byng's Third Army joined in on 20 October with a night attack at 0200hrs. The Selle was crossed with little difficulty, and by nightfall the forward troops were digging in on the high ground to the east. A two-day pause allowed Byng to bring his artillery forwards before launching a combined attack with Fourth Army on 24 October which drove as far as the Forest of Mormal 13km to the east, having taken 7,300 prisoners.

The high number of prisoners indicated the increasingly fragile state of the German Army following its defeat on the Hindenburg Line. As the news of the Armistice request percolated through the German Army, postal censors noted

British troops advancing to the Selle in Albion lorries near Joncourt on 9 October 1918. (IWM, Q9530)

that there had been a significant downturn in the troops' motivation to fight on; they now wanted peace. They no longer believed in the national leadership and discipline evaporated in parts of the army. This factor had a defining influence on both the Allied and German political and military leaderships as they developed their positions on the Armistice request.

As early as 10 October, Foch had outlined his recommendations to Haig that the Germans should be required to evacuate Belgium, France and Alsace-Lorraine; military equipment was to be abandoned, and the west bank of the Rhine passed into Allied administration along with bridgeheads east of the river. Although Haig suggested that this was akin to an unconditional surrender, Foch believed that the German situation was now so critical that more moderate terms were no longer necessary. The dialogue between Germany and Washington had initially raised hopes in Berlin that Alsace-Lorraine could be retained, but the sinking of the SS *Leinster* on 12 October by a German submarine, with the loss of 450 civilian lives, hardened President Wilson's stance. Two days later he stipulated that the Armistice conditions must guarantee Allied military supremacy and implied that the Kaiser should be removed from power.

On 16 October, Foch met with Clemenceau. Both were aware of the erosion of France's strength and the consequent weakening of their position at the peace settlement if the war was extended. However, with intelligence decrypts illustrating the level of disintegration in Germany, they agreed to hold a hard line based on Foch's terms. The next day, the German cabinet met to determine whether they could improve their position by prolonging the fight. Ludendorff now suggested that the Allies were reaching the limit of their offensive power and that the German manpower and oil situation was not as bad as first feared. But the politicians in the Reichstag had now lost confidence in OHL, and Ludendorff's advice was not heeded; President Wilson's stipulations were agreed. Despite the success of their armies, the British position was moderating its terms but also wanted a quick termination of the fighting. Lloyd George's Cabinet met on 19 October, when Haig informed them that logistical difficulties and the fast-approaching winter necessitated a more moderate approach to secure the Armistice before the Germans could rehabilitate their army with new recruits. As the manpower situation remained critical, the British politicians decided that extending the fighting would only strengthen the American position in the negotiations and concurred with Haig.

Notwithstanding British and French concerns over America's growing influence, on 22 October, President Wilson was advised by his Cabinet that the growing military dominance of the British and French over the Germans would only strengthen their hand in the peace settlement if the war dragged on. Fearing the consequent empowerment of the British and French Empires, the next day he sent a note to Berlin making it clear that any Armistice agreement must be based on Foch's demands and make a return to conflict impossible. Furthermore, concessions were given to Britain to uphold their objection to Wilson's 'freedom of the seas' proposal, in order to gain their assent to the Armistice. Thus, making very different assessments of the relative powers of the Allied and German forces, all three of the major Allied powers concluded that the war should be brought to a halt as soon as possible, and that despite ongoing differences, Belgium, France and Alsace-Lorraine would need to be evacuated, and French security guaranteed.

The consequences of Wilson's note in Germany were seismic. On 24 October, Hindenburg and Ludendorff sent a telegram to the armies stating that the fight must go on to prevent the destruction of Germany. The telegram, however, had not been authorized by either the Kaiser or Prinz Max, who threatened to resign as a result. Two days later Hindenburg and Ludendorff travelled to Berlin without permission for a dénouement. After a furious exchange, the Kaiser reprimanded both for their insubordinate behaviour and inconsistent advice. Hindenburg and Ludendorff tendered their resignations as they had done before. This time the Kaiser accepted Ludendorff's offer; Hindenburg was ordered to stay. For two weeks the Kaiser hung on to power, although he decamped from Berlin to Spa. However, the Armistice shockwaves reverberated around Germany. On 4 November the High Seas Fleet mutinied at Kiel in the face of a suicidal sortie into the North Sea being planned. The revolt quickly spread across Germany, and as the Government struggled to keep control, the Social Democratic Party leadership made Wilhelm's abdication a condition of their continued support. Consequently, on 9 November, Prinz Max announced his removal from the Imperial and Prussian thrones. The Kaiser briefly toyed with the idea of leading a military force back to Berlin to restore his authority, but Hindenburg advised that the army would no longer follow him and suggested that he leave for exile in Holland. Wilhelm made the trip on 10 November and Germany became a republic; the Armistice was signed the following day.

Ludendorff's authority had been built on battlefield success at Liège, Tannenburg, Gorlice-Tarnow and the defensive battles of 1916–17. The tide turned against him when his offensive strategy collapsed in July 1918, but the *coup de grâce* was applied on the Hindenburg Line. The battle was a defeat for the German Army, but it set in motion forces that shattered the German political establishment and set the broad timetable and shape of the peace that followed.

The processes that removed the battle from public awareness were in action even as events unfolded on the battlefields. By late 1917, Lloyd George had lost so much faith in his military leaders that he began a concerted attempt to convince his political colleagues and the public of the benefits of his 'Eastern' strategy. In February 1918, the newspaper magnates Lord Beaverbrook and Lord Northcliffe were respectively made Minister for Information and Director of the Department of Propaganda in Enemy Countries. Their mutually supporting briefs were to control public perceptions of the conduct of the war. From the Spring Offensive it became apparent that the narrative towards the British Army would be negative. Accusations of cowardice in Fifth Army in March helped the Government

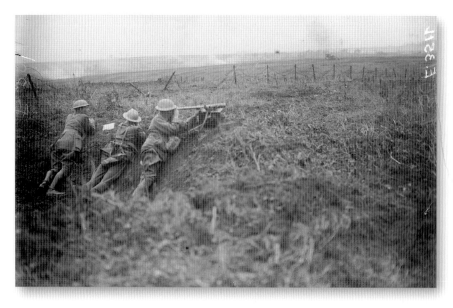

Australian Press Correspondents Bean, Murdoch and Gilmour watching an attack. (IWM, E(AUS) 3511)

limit its own culpability. Beaverbrook pushed articles that championed successes in the Middle East and the build-up of the American Army in the West to highlight the Government's developing policy. The situation was not helped by GHQ's antipathy towards the Press and vastly improved operational security measures, both of which made the reporting of combat more difficult. When the Press did visit the BEF, Beaverbrook directed them towards the Dominion forces. The final ignominy was official congratulations from the War Cabinet to Allenby in Palestine and Pershing in France for their victories in late September. The absence of similar laurels for Haig and his armies did not go unnoticed.

Notwithstanding the vicissitudes of the Press, another major factor was that the BEF did not fully understand the character of its victories. Its pre-war and wartime doctrines were framed around tactics and strategy, but there was no conceptual reference point for what became known later as the 'operational level of war'. In grappling with this problem, Haig and his men operated beyond the contemporary understanding of their profession. That they did so successfully was an immense achievement, but in the face of new conflicts around the globe and post-war financial retrenchment at home, the British General Staff struggled to institutionalize it as new doctrine. Although Field Service Regulations were redrafted four times between 1918 and 1935, they reached no higher than tactics for large formations. The dislocation of the German reserves was unknown in this period and only disclosed when the 1918 volume of the German Official History was published in 1944. Being submerged by the climactic events of the next war, this factor consequently went un-noticed by the British Official History volumes for August–November 1918 which were published in 1947. The movement of German Divisions was partially – but inaccurately – recorded and being split between the final two volumes, the nuance of the period between late August and late September in this respect was lost.

Because of these complex circumstances, the BEF's successes on the Hindenburg Line were never properly recorded or fully understood in the first instance, and unsurprisingly, they rapidly vanished from the cultural memory of the war.

THE BATTLEFIELD TODAY

As the armies left, so the population returned to the region to repair their towns and villages and restore the agricultural economy. Rolling fields of wheat and sugar beet greet the visitor today, with the rivers and canals gently flowing through the rolling downland. Although the barbed wire was cleared and the trenches filled in, the reinforced concrete bunkers proved more resilient relics. Being difficult to destroy, the local farmers initially worked around them, and until recently, when the fields were not in crop, the path of the Hindenburg Line could be easily traced. However, the damage they did to expensive farm machinery meant they became less tolerable, and as the Superintendent of Bony American Cemetery informed the author, many are now being demolished. Away from farmland they can still be found, particularly along the banks of the canal towpaths. Similarly, where the trench lines cut through woods and copses, their weathered vestiges can sometimes still be seen. The canals and bridges themselves also remain, particularly the bridge at Riqueval captured spectacularly by 46th Division on 29 September. More movingly, from place to place the visitor will come across the carefully tended cemeteries containing those who lost their lives in the fighting. Many of the British and Dominion cemeteries are relatively small, such as those at Sequehart, with the men being buried in the places where they fell as the battle passed through. The American troops were mostly centralized into the large cemetery at Bony, marking the sacrifices of II (US) Corps. The German dead can be found in the large cemeteries at Maissemy, St Quentin, Le Cateau and Cambrai, while those of the French lie in the St Quentin Necropole National. Other monuments were constructed after the war, with that commemorating II (US) Corps at Bellicourt providing panoramic views across the battlefield south of Bony. More discretely, the 4th Australian Division memorial overlooking Bellenglise marks the Advanced Hindenburg Line, seized on 18 September at the battle of Épehy and also the line of departure for IX Corps' assault on 29 September.

The memorial to II (US) Corps at Bellicourt. (Author)

The Hindenburg Line battlefield is an order of magnitude bigger than the majority of those from earlier in the war. Palluel on the Sensée is 60km from Berthenicourt on the Oise, while approximately 15km separates the Canal du Nord and the St Quentin Canal from the final positions taken east of Cambrai and at Prémont; transport is therefore essential if the visitor wishes to fully appreciate the geographic scale of the campaign. Access is straightforward for British visitors, as the A26 Autoroute from Calais passes along the Hindenburg Outpost Line between Cambrai and St Quentin. Paris is approximately

130km to the south for those flying in from elsewhere in the globe. There are far fewer visitors to this battlefield than to the Somme, and there are no equivalents of the museums such as those at Thiepval or Delville Wood. La Historial de la Grande Guerre at Péronne is around 20km west of Bellenglise. It is an exceptional institution that promotes reflection of the events of 1914–18. With respect to the battles in 1918 it has an outstanding light projection display of the Australian Corps' seizure of Mont St Quentin in August. As an illustration of the tactical flexibility and manoeuvrability of the BEF in 1918 it is unmatched.

The achievement of the BEF in this pivotal battle has never received the acclaim it deserves. At the limits of national resource and at frontier of contemporary military thought, alongside its Allies The BEF outgeneralled, outmanoeuvred and ultimately outfought its German adversary. It is hoped that this book will help the forgotten victory of Haig and the BEF to re-emerge from the shadows.

FURTHER READING

Badsey, S., *The British Army in Battle and its Image 1914–1918*, Continuum: London, 2014

Bean, C. E. W., *Official History of Australia in the Great War, Vol VI, The AIF in France 1918*, Angus and Robertson: Sydney, 1942

Boff, J., *Winning and Losing on the Western Front*, Cambridge University Press: Cambridge, 2012

Der Weltkrieg 1914–1918: die miltärischen Operationen zu Lande, Vol 14, Die Kriegführung der Westfront im Jahre 1918, Mittler und Sohn: Berlin, 1944

Die Bayern im Grossen Kriege 1914–1918, Bayerischen Kriegsarchiv: Munich, 1923

Edmonds, J. E., *History of the Great War, Military Operations France and Belgium 1918, Vol IV, 8th August–26th September, The Franco-British Offensive*, Battery Press: Nashville, 1993

Edmonds, J. E., *History of the Great War, Military Operations France and Belgium 1918, Vol V, 26th September–11th November, The Advance to Victory, The Franco-British Offensive*, Battery Press: Nashville, 1993

French, D., *The Strategy of the Lloyd George Coalition, 1916–1918*, Clarendon Press: Oxford, 1995

Greenhalgh, E., *Foch in Command: The Forging of a First World War General*, Cambridge University Press: Cambridge, 2011

Harris, J. P. with Barr, N., *Amiens to the Armistice*, Brassey: London 1998

Jones, H. A., *The War in the Air, Vol VI*, Oxford University Press: Oxford: 1937

Les Armées Francaises dans la Grande Guerre, Tome VII, Ire Vol, Impremerie Nationale: Paris, 1923

Les Armées Francaises dans la Grande Guerre, Tome VII, IIeme Vol, Impremerie Nationale: Paris, 1938

Nicholson, G. W. L., *Canadian Expeditionary Force 1914–1918: Official History of the Canadian Army in the Great War*, Roger Duhamel: Ottawa, 1962

Prior, R. and Wilson, T., *Command on the Western Front: The Military Career of Sir Henry Rawlinson 1914–1918*, Leo Cooper: Barnsley, 2004

Sheffield, G., *Forgotten Victory*, Headline: London, 2001

Sheffield, G. and Bourne, J., *Douglas Haig: War Diaries and Letters 1914–1918*, Weidenfeld and Nicholson: London, 2005

Simpson, A., *Directing Operations: British Corps Command on the Western Front*, Spellmount: Stroud, 2006

Stevenson, D., *With Our Backs to the Wall: Victory and Defeat in 1918*, Allen Lane: London, 2011

Tooze, A., *The Deluge; the Great War and the Remaking of Global Order*, Allen Lane: London, 2015

Yokelson M. A., *Borrowed Soldiers: Americans under British Command, 1918*, University of Oklahoma Press: Norman, 2008

Numerous British, German, French, Australian and Canadian War Diaries, Divisional and Regimental histories